THOUGHTS

ON

PHYSICAL EDUCATION, &c.

THOUGHTS

ON

PHYSICAL EDUCATION,

AND

THE TRUE MODE OF IMPROVING THE CONDITION OF MAN;

AND ON THE

STUDY OF THE GREEK AND LATIN LANGUAGES.

By CHARLES CALDWELL, M. D.,

PROFESSOR OF THE INSTITUTES OF MEDICINE AND CLINICAL PRACTICE
IN TRANSYLVANIA UNIVERSITY.

WITH NOTES BY ROBERT COX,

AND

A RECOMMENDATORY PREFACE

By GEORGE COMBE.

EDINBURGH:
ADAM & CHARLES BLACK, NORTH BRIDGE STREET
AND LONGMAN & CO., LONDON.

MDCCCXXXVI.

PRINTED BY NEILL & CO., OLD FISHMARKET, EDINBURGH.

INTRODUCTORY REMARKS.

In presenting Dr Caldwell's "Thoughts on Physical Education" to the English reader, it is almost superfluous to offer any preliminary recommendation. Dr Caldwell is well known as one of the most clear, forcible, and eloquent writers in the United States; and he is as much distinguished for the depth and soundness of his philosophical views, as for his great talent in expounding them. In the present work, he takes a comprehensive and just survey of human nature, embracing at once its physical, moral, and intellectual aspects, and shews the influence of physical training on them all. Under the general term Education, two very distinguishable processes are very often confounded,—namely, *training* and *instruction*. Training, in reference to education, means the strengthening and improving, by means of exercise, the mental functions, thereby increasing their agility and capacity; while instruction refers to the communication of knowledge. Dr Caldwell's work is limited to the first, or training: and it is important to keep this fact steadily in view, that his reasoning may not be misapprehended. He regards education as a scheme of action by which any living being may be improved, and, by perseverance, raised to the highest perfection of which it is susceptible. The organized system of man constitutes the machinery by means of which his mind operates during life. Every one, says he, admits that the legs and arms may be strengthened and rendered more agile by means of judicious exercise; and most persons acknowledge that the external senses also may be improved by similar means. The savage, whose ear is cultivated as the means of his safety, hears sounds that are inaudible to a civilized European. But the effect produced in these instances, results entirely from an improvement *in the condition of the organs*. The same may be affirmed with equal safety respecting the higher mental operations. In performing these, the mind operates by means of the brain, as certainly as it does by the eye in seeing, and by the muscles in dancing or fencing. When any form of memory, or the power of reasoning, is increased by judicious training, the mind itself is not changed; the improvement, in this as in the preceding cases, is confined to the organs by the aid of which the mind remembers and reasons. Physical education, therefore, lies at the foundation of all successful training, both bodily and mental.

Dr Caldwell remarks, that the most philosophical and useful manner of viewing physical education, would be to regard it as a process for training the different parts of our corporeal system to their highest state of attainable perfection, each according to its own constitution and functions. The skin, for example, must be treated by one mode of discipline; the stomach by another; and the lungs by a third. And, in like manner, if the feelings common to man and the lower animals are connected with one portion of the brain, the moral sentiments with a second, and the intellectual powers with a third, it is necessary to train each of these separately, by means adapted to the nature of the function, and to the object which we have in view, whether this be to repress or to exalt its energy; and we shall err and suffer disappointment if we attempt to educate the whole mind by one process, by whatever name we may designate it. " The condition of the morals of every individual," says he, " depends on the condition of the moral organs of his brain,—the condition of his intellect on that of his intellectual organs, —and the condition of his physical powers on that of the remaining portion of his body"—including the skin, digestive viscera, lungs, heart, muscles, and the organs of secretion and absorption. All these parts, he observes, are so mutually dependent, that no one of them can be either materially injured or benefited alone. If the digestive, respiratory, and circulatory systems, or either of them, is seriously deranged, the brain suffers for want of a sufficient supply of good blood to nourish, vivify, and strengthen it. If the brain itself is materially deranged, it is incompetent to prepare, in due quantity, and of sound qualities, the nervous influence of which the other parts of the system constantly stand in need; and therefore they suffer in turn. "Hence," he adds, " moral and intellectual education, which consists in amending the condition of the brain, and physical education, which is the improvement of the other parts of the body, are indispensable to the perfection of each other, and of course to that of the whole system. Physical education is to the other two, what the root, trunk, and branches of the tree are to its leaves, blossoms, and fruit. It is the source and *sine qua non* of their existence. Injure or improve it, and you produce on them a kindred effect. Hence physical education is far more important than is commonly imagined. Without a due regard to it, by which I mean a stricter and more judicious attention than is paid to it at present, man cannot attain the perfection of his nature. Ancient Greece might be cited in confirmation of this. May history and other forms of record be credited, the people of that country were, as a nation, physically and intellectually, the most perfect of the human race. And there is reason to believe, that their unrivalled attention to physical education was highly influential in producing the result."

These views are followed up in the work itself, in a very able, lucid, and practical manner; the principle on which every precept is founded, and the consequences of obeying or disobeying it, are presented in such close and striking connexion, that it is impossible to read the book without interest, or to lay it down without desiring to reduce it to practice. It forms a valuable addition to a class of writings which have of late acquired great popularity both in this country and in America, including such works as that of Dr Brigham on the Influence of Mental Cultivation and Mental Excitement upon Health, and Dr Combe on Physiology applied to Health and Education, and on Digestion. I can safely recommend it in the highest terms to public attention. The treatise, it is proper to state, was originally published at Boston, U. S., in 1834, in a volume with this title—" Thoughts on Physical Education: Being a Discourse delivered to a Convention of Teachers in Lexington, Kentucky, on the 6th and 7th of November 1833."

The second treatise from the pen of Dr Caldwell, here reprinted, is entitled, " Thoughts on the Study of the Greek and Latin Languages." It refers directly to the second element of Education, namely *instruction*. It was published several years ago in the New England Magazine. The subject is one which has recently excited great attention in this country, and Dr Caldwell discusses it in a masterly style. The grand question is, whether the works of nature, proceeding directly from the Creator, and adapted by him to the human faculties,—or two dead languages, Greek and Latin, artificial inventions at the first, and long disused by all living nations, form the better objects for stimulating, strengthening, and enlightening the intellectual powers, and for humanizing the feelings of the young. Dr Caldwell takes the side of Nature, and defends her claims with much eloquence, energy, and learning. He does not, however, absolutely exclude Greek and Latin from the list of profitable studies; his whole aim is to destroy that absurd and superstitious reverence for these languages, which substitutes them for science, and wastes the precious years of youth in acquiring a knowledge of mere words and abstractions in prosody and grammar, instead of becoming acquainted with creation. To those individuals who have a taste for languages, and have leisure to embrace them in their studies, no object probably can be more interesting and attractive than Greek and Roman literature; and to this class of students Dr Caldwell proposes to leave all their enjoyments unimpaired.

The present volume is edited by Mr ROBERT COX, who, besides adding numerous notes and an Index, has enriched the Treatise on Physical Education by introducing into the text select passages from other essays published in a detached form by Dr Caldwell—especially his " Thoughts on the True

Mode of Improving the Condition of Man," nearly the whole of which has been amalgamated with the present work. No addition has been made to the treatise on the Study of the Greek and Latin Languages.

GEO. COMBE.

23. CHARLOTTE SQUARE,
EDINBURGH, 26th May 1836.

PREFACE

TO THE

AMERICAN EDITION.

The following production, being too long for a Discourse and too short for a Treatise, and possessing neither the style nor the manner of an Essay, is a sort of nondescript in form, and by a certain class of readers will perhaps, at first sight, be considered no less so in some of the sentiments it contains. Should it be favoured, however, with an attentive perusal, and a few second and serious thoughts, it is hoped that a more familiar acquaintance with it will wear off any disagreeable effects that first impressions may have produced.

The author was induced to prepare and deliver it, and has been led to print it for sundry reasons. He was requested to do so, and did not think it kind or complaisant to refuse. The subject is one of great importance, involving the highest perfection and earthly happiness that man can attain, to say nothing of its bearing on his future condition—and it has rarely, if ever, been treated on the ground, and under the extent of principle, that justly belong to it. But the chief reason for publishing the work, was a belief that it contains a few seminal truths, not generally known, which, when fully developed and reduced to practice, will lead to results of much usefulness in the work of education.

The subject is treated altogether *physiologically*; and that such is the nature of education cannot be denied. Every change it produces in those who are made the subject of it is strictly physiological. This is as true of moral and intellectual as of physical education. All the beneficial effects of training arise from the improvements produced by it in organized matter, rendering such matter, whether it be brain, nerve, muscle, lungs, or of any other description, a better piece of machinery for mind to work with. A knowledge of these truths is peculiarly important, as they show the essential connexion between mind and matter, and make it clearly appear, that, for its sound and vigorous operations, the former depends on the condition of the latter. Hence the importance of a strict attention to the health of pupils, even independently of their corporeal suffering from disease. Their mental character is no less concerned in the issue.

Let no one allege that this view of education involves materialism, or any principle unfriendly to morality or religion. The charge would be most unjust. The entire subserviency of matter to mind is acknowledged in it; and that is all that the doctrine of spirituality can require. It must not claim to take from matter the rank and attributes conferred on it by its CREATOR; but for a fuller discussion of these topics, the reader is referred to the work itself, which, without further remark, is respectfully submitted to his unprejudiced judgment.

THOUGHTS

ON

PHYSICAL EDUCATION, &c.

Gentlemen,

It would not only be a departure from the object that has called you together, but objectionable in itself and injurious in its effects, to introduce into the exercises of the present occasion the slightest allusion to matters of party. Nor would any one more reluctantly than myself be guilty of such a fault. Let me hope, however, that, without furnishing ground for a charge against me to that effect, or awakening in the mind of any one who hears me an unfriendly feeling or an opposing thought, I may be permitted to observe, that the aspect of our country, political as well as social, is gloomy and portentous. And when we turn from the present to the future, the prospect presents but little to cheer us, unless a change, to be presently specified, can be produced in the public mind. While the embittered strife of parties, differing in their views of men and measures, and the growing discontents of geographical sections,* seriously threaten the repose of the country, not to say the integrity of the Union,—the poison spread abroad by malice and false-

---

* This Discourse was written at the time when the spirit of NULLIFICATION in the South was at its height.

hood, through the public prints, is tainting the community with moral corruption. So deep and pestilent is this fountain, and so broad and destructive to soundness of principle, as well as to the love and diffusion of truth, the stream that issues from it, as to render it perhaps more than doubtful, whether, perverted as it is to the vilest of purposes, the freedom of the press be a good or an evil. If men be too corrupt and vicious to refrain, of their own accord, from practices disgraceful in themselves and ruinous to their country, I am far from being convinced that they ought not to be debarred from them by public authority.

Every excess is an evil; and that of the liberty of the press, which, turned to licentiousness, defames, misleads, inflames, and demoralizes, is among the most deplorable. Were any one to pronounce the sentiment here advanced to be unfriendly to the doctrines of republican government, my reply would be, that it is not unfriendly to morality or Christianity, but concurrent with both. Nor is it less so with the spirit of genuine republicanism, which embraces and upholds the *general good*, and is therefore hostile to the corruption, fraud, and falsehood, to which too many of our public presses unblushingly minister.

For this condition of things, stored with the elements of such fearful calamity, there is but one remedy—*the advancement of the people in intelligence and virtue.* I say "advancement;" for there is reason to apprehend that the stock of those attributes now possessed by us is too limited for the work to be performed by them—the eradication of existing, and the prevention of future and more grievous evils. It is to the improved mental character of the rising generation, and those who shall succeed them, beyond that of the generation now at maturity, that our hopes can attach themselves with any reasonable prospect of being realized. On the redeeming influence of such improvement alone can the American people safely and confidently rely for the attainment of that degree of national prosperity, greatness, and glory, and that amount of individual happiness, which is placed within their reach if they do not neglect or abuse their privileges.

Two questions of moment here present themselves. Is the amendment referred to within our reach? and if so, what are the means by which it may be compassed? I answer, Yes: the end can be attained; and *an improved education constitutes the means*. To represent it fairly, and recommend it to the acceptance and encouragement it deserves, I may safely add that it is the only means. To rely on any other would be a *deadly* fallacy. By that alone can our safety be secured; and by that it *can* be secured, provided we avail ourselves of it as wisdom dictates and duty enjoins. But we must avail ourselves of it promptly, else the opportunity may be lost to us for ever. It is not only " in the affairs of *men*" that " there is a tide which, taken at the flood, leads on to fortune;" the same is no less true of *nations*. And I may truly add, " On such a full sea are we now afloat; and we must take the current as it serves, or lose our venture."

The influence of education on the condition of our country, were it judiciously conducted and generally diffused, would be irresistible; and its issue would be precisely the improvement we require. Not only would the people receive from it the intelligence necessary to guide them in public affairs; they would be improved by it in their entire character, moral and social, intellectual and political, and enabled the better to control their passions, and give them a safe and useful direction. Prepared to perceive the public good with greater clearness, and to pursue it with purer intentions and a steadier aim, they would be less susceptible of the rage and sway of party, and more effectually guarded against the machinations of unprincipled demagogues and aspirants to power, who might wish to mislead them for the promotion of their own selfish and sinister purposes. Thus would the nation become a nursery of abler statesmen and more virtuous patriots, and have its highest interests more certainly secured.

Fortunately for our country these sentiments are not

new; nor are they limited as respects the number of those who entertain them. They are taking root in the public mind with the most gratifying rapidity, and promise to be productive of invaluable fruit. There is reason to hope, that, as the issue of them, education will be no longer neglected in the United States, but improved and extended in proportion to our demand for it. Already is the interest awakened in favour of it broad and deep; and it is beginning to be regarded in its true character, as constituting not only the corner-stone but the foundation and cement of civil society. Already is it beginning to be looked to, as alone calculated to rescue human nature from the dominion of animal propensity and passion, and to bestow on it the highest perfection of which it is susceptible. Uneducated whites, and the roving children of the forest, will soon be considered, and justly so, as occupying nearly the same level in the scale of being. Nor is this all. There is cause to believe that the period is approaching when to be wholly uneducated will be held dishonourable and out of fashion; and that will do much to complete the spread and triumph of education. As respects the points on which they bear, honour and fashion are every where despotic.

That these views are not fallacious, but that the salutary change referred to is in progress, appears from an abundance of concurrent testimony. The meeting of the Convention I have the honour of addressing, testifies strongly to that effect. So do many other facts, which might be easily cited. Teachers of every rank in their profession are not only better rewarded, but held in higher estimation than formerly. It is no longer true, as it once was, that persons unfit for any thing else on account of indolence, infirmity, or some other disqualification, are employed as instructors. Men of character and competency alone are now considered worthy of the trust. Already is this the case in many parts of our country, and promises soon to be so in all of them. Annals, journals, and libraries are established, lyceums are opened, institutes erected, associations formed, essays published, sermons preached, conventions held, and discourses delivered, for the advancement of education. Those measures are calculated to form, foster, and diffuse a taste for it, excite ambition in it, and, rendering it popular, insure its success. For popularity, whether it attach to projects fitted for good or for evil, is a current which nothing can withstand; and, fortunately, in the present instance, it sets in the right direction. In fine, a large portion of the talent of America being in some way enlisted in the cause of education, and the general bent of society concurring with it, an effort so powerful and well directed can scarcely fail to produce an era in the annals of our country, memorable alike for the diffusion of useful knowledge and the advancement of human happiness. In the vocabulary of such numbers, united and resolute, intelligent and persevering, there is no suitable place for the terms *impossibility*, *failure*, or *defeat*. To confederacies of the kind, all things within the scope of human means become practicable and easy. But my business is not to speak of education in the abstract, but to offer a few remarks on one of its branches. To that task I shall now proceed.

That I may the more easily and certainly be understood, however, in my subsequent exposition of it, allow me first to make a few observations explanatory of what I mean by the term *education*, as my understanding of it may differ, perhaps, in some degree from yours. Any theoretical difference, however, that may exist between us on this point, will have no influence in creating a practical one on others of more immediate usefulness.

Let me here apprise you, that, in giving my definition, I must speak phrenologically. As education relates to the operations of mind as well as of body, it must be considered and presented, as well summarily as in detail, with a reference to some system of mental philosophy. But of all the systems I have examined, (and I have looked carefully into several of them,) that of Gall and Spurzheim is the only one I can either believe or understand. As soon would I bind myself to discover the philosopher's stone, or to concoct the elixir of life out of simples, as to find substantial meaning in many of the tenets of fashionable metaphysics. Indeed, the dreams of alchymists, and not a few of those of metaphysicians, have a strong family-likeness. And well they may. They are the twin-brood of common parents, error and superstition, and were ushered to life during the dark ages. These are my reasons for speaking in conformity to phrenological principles, in the definition I am about to offer.

By education, in the abstract, I mean *a scheme of action or training, by which any form of living matter may be improved, and, by perseverance, reared to the highest perfection of which it is susceptible.* I say "any form;" because the lower orders of living beings, vegetables not excepted, may be educated and improved, as certainly as the higher, and on the same grounds. That it may produce the desired effect, the scheme pursued must conform to the constitution of the race of beings for whose improvement it is intended; and, in the present instance, that race is our own. No one, therefore, is capable of devising and arranging such a scheme for the amendment of the general condition of man, or even of comprehending and skilfully applying it, unless he be thoroughly acquainted with his constitution. Hence, without such an acquaintance, it is impossible to become an able and successful instructor. He that would rectify or improve a piece of machinery, must first understand it in its structure and principles. Under the want of such a knowledge of it, to touch it is to impair it, except it be saved by the intervention of accident. In like manner, he that would alter human nature for the better must know it *as it is.* Special education, designed for a given purpose, is a scheme of training in accordance with that purpose. I need scarcely add, that general training does nothing more than improve general powers; while special training fits for some definite and corresponding pursuit.

By the constitution of man, as just referred to, I mean

his material portion, in its organized and vital capacity; that being, as I feel persuaded, the only part of him *we* are able to improve. The mind being a spirit, whose nature and qualities *as spirit* are concealed from us, and with which none of our faculties is fitted to make us acquainted, we do not possess any means, nor can we conceive of any, calculated to produce in it either amendment or change. Its subtle and inscrutable character places it beyond our action and influence. Nor, as will appear hereafter, does the work of education require it to be changed. It only calls for an amendment of the instruments with which it works. So exalted is my view of spirit, that I believe it to be competent, without any interference from us, to the highest actions for which the body is fitted. To amend it belongs only to HIM who made it.

It occurs to me, that he who believes in his power to improve spirit, by making it stronger, larger, more active, or in any respect better, has a much less exalted opinion of it than he has of himself. A capacity to amend implies a superiority in the amender and his machinery to the thing he improves. But the whole machinery of education is material. To contend, then, that education can improve *the abstract mind,* is to assert *the superiority of matter to spirit.* This is neither quibble nor sophistry, but a deduction of reason, and a dictate of common sense. Nor will any thing but a spirit of sophistry attempt its subversion. Except the teacher be superior to the pupil, he cannot instruct him. Much less can he do so, being greatly inferior. Spirit, being the superior, *may* modify and amend matter; but for the converse of this to be true, seems impossible.

The organized system of man constitutes the machinery with which alone his mind operates, during their connexion as soul and body. Improve the apparatus, then, and you facilitate and improve the work which the mind performs with it, precisely as you facilitate steam operation, and enhance its product, by improving the machinery with which it is executed. In one case, steam, and in the other, spirit, continue unchanged; and each works and produces with a degree of perfection corresponding to that of the instruments it employs.

As respects several of the functions of the mind, the correctness of the foregoing theory is universally admitted. Seeing, hearing, tasting, smelling, and feeling, as well as voluntary muscular motion, are as true mental operations as judging, reasoning, remembering, or calculation by numbers. And the former are as susceptible of improvement as the latter. But when improved, no one considers the result as consisting in any amendment of simple spirit, but of compound organized matter. When, for example, vision is improved, the amendment is uniformly referred to the eye, the optic nerve, and that portion of the brain immediately associated with them; they being the organs by which the mind sees, and without which it cannot see. Is hearing improved? For the same reason, it is not the mind, but the auditory apparatus, that is amended. Of the other senses, the same is true. If either of them be improved, it is the organ that is meliorated in its condition, not the mind that uses it. Nor is this truth less obvious as respects the instruments of voluntary motion. The opera-dancer, the tumbler, and the swordsman, do not, in acquiring expertness in their occupations, improve their minds, but their muscles and joints, with the nerves and portions of the brain that have the governance of them. These positions are so plain, that to state them is to prove them.

Respecting the higher mental operations, the same may be affirmed with equal safety. In performing them, the mind works with the brain as its machinery, as certainly as it does with the eye in seeing, or the muscles in dancing and swordsmanship. Is any form of memory —say the memory of words, or that of places—rendered more apt and retentive by judicious exercise? We have no reason to believe that the mind or spirit is amended in this instance, any more than in those heretofore enumerated. It is a portion of the brain—the organ of language or locality—that is amended. By practice, man becomes more powerful and adroit in reasoning and judging. Here, again, the mind is not changed. The belief to that effect has no shadow of evidence to sustain it. The improvement in this case, as in the preceding ones, is confined to the organs with which the mind reasons and judges. Arguments, not to be refuted, could be adduced in favour of this statement, were the discussion admissible. Indeed, for man to claim the power of operating immediately on spirit, and either amending or deteriorating it, by any means he can employ, is an assumption perfectly gratuitous, and, in my opinion, not a little extraordinary and arrogant. It is enough that he is able to change matter, and control it to his purposes, *by material agents.* And all the means used in teaching *are* material. There is good reason to believe, as already stated, that nothing short of the CREATIVE WILL that brought spirit into existence can modify it, either for better or worse. When we wish, then, I say, to improve mental operations, *we have only to amend the organs which the mind employs in performing them.* And it will appear hereafter, that this is a proposition of great importance in the scheme of human improvement. For no other reason would I have ventured to introduce it on the present occasion, aware, as I am, that its correctness is not likely at first to be generally acknowledged by you. Allow me, however, to repeat, that a difference of opinion on this point will have no tendency to create a difference on many that are to follow. The difference will be in theory, not in practice.

Education is usually divided into two branches, physical and moral. More correctly might it be divided into three—physical, moral, and intellectual. Nothing is more certain, than that the intellectual and the moral powers may be educated separately; the former being amended while the latter are not, and the converse. Facts in proof of this are abundant. There is as real a distinction between moral and intellectual education, as there is between physical education and either of them. It will appear, however, presently, that they are all three so intimately connected, that the improvement of any one of them may be made to contribute to that of the others. Nor can it be otherwise, except through mismanagement. Moral action, intellectual action, and what, for want of a better name, I may call physical action, have their seats and instruments in different parts of the human system; and those parts are essentially connected by sympathy, and other ties more mechanical and obvious. One of them being injured or benefited, therefore, the others are affected in a corresponding manner. Deriving their being and sustenance from the same source, and serving as elements of the same individual person, each of whose parts is necessary to the integrity and perfection of the whole, it would be singular were it not so. To illustrate my meaning, and prove my position:—

The condition of the morals of every individual depends on the condition of the moral organs of his brain,—the condition of his intellect on that of his intellectual organs,—and the condition of his physical powers on that of the remaining portion of his body. The human body is a very complicated apparatus. It consists of many different organs, which are again made up of other organs, each performing its specific functions. But these organs, I repeat, instead of acting every one for itself alone, act also for each other individually and collectively, and are united in a system by function and sympathy. The condition of one organ, therefore, whether sound or unsound, influences and modifies that of many others. If it be a principal organ, it influences the whole machine. There are three great sets of organs, which, while they are intimately and indispensably connected with each other, control all the rest, and assimilate their condition in no small degree to their own. These are the chylopoëtic (chyle-making or digestive) organs,—the blood-making and blood-circulating organs, consisting of the lungs and the heart,—and the brain, spinal cord, and nerves, which are the instruments of intellect and feeling, and are essential also to voluntary motion. To the heart must be added its appendages, the bloodvessels. These three sets of organs have been said to control all the others; and this they do chiefly by mutually controlling themselves—by exercising, I mean, such a reciprocal influence as to be all at the same time somewhat assimilated in condition. They are as necessary to each other as they are to the whole. Is one of them materially deranged in its action? The two others suffer immediately, and all the rest of the system in its turn. Is the brain diseased? Its healthy influence, which is indispensable to the well-being of the two other sets of associated organs, is withheld from them, and they also fail in their action, as well as in their sound and sustaining sympathies. The chyle and blood are deteriorated. This proves a source of further injury to the brain, which, unless it be supplied with well prepared blood, is neither itself in good condition, nor capable of contributing to the health and efficiency of the other parts of the body. It cannot prepare, from a scanty and bad material, the substance or agent of its own influence, whatever it may be, in sufficient quantity, and of sound qualities. The general mischief arising from a primary morbid affection of either of the two other sets of controlling organs, is equally demonstrable, and depends on similar principles. But it is needless to dwell longer on this subject. To every physiologist it is already familiar. It is known to him, that out of chyle of bad qualities, or deficient in quantity, a sufficient amount of good blood cannot be prepared; that if respiration be defective, the latter fluid cannot be duly vitalized; and that if the heart be enfeebled, it cannot throw the blood with the requisite force into every part of the system. Hence I repeat, that moral and intellectual education, which consists in amending the condition of the brain, and physical education, which is the improvement of the other parts of the body, are indispensable to the perfection of each other, and of course to that of the whole system. Physical education is to the other two what the root, trunk, and branches of the tree are to its leaves, blossoms, and fruit. It is the source and *sine qua non* of their existence. Injure or improve it, and you produce on them a kindred effect. Hence, physical education is far more important than is commonly imagined. Without a due regard to it, by which I mean a stricter and more judicious attention than is paid to it at present, man cannot attain the perfection of his nature. Ancient Greece might be cited in confirmation of this. May history and other forms of record be credited, the people of that country were, as a nation, physically and intellectually the most perfect of the human race. And there is reason to believe, that their unrivalled attention to physical education was highly influential in producing the result.

In truth, the ancient Persians and Greeks, as well as some other nations of antiquity, appear to have cultivated that form of education to a much greater extent than the moderns do. Nor were they without their reasons for this. For their standing in war, in common with their influence in peace, individuals among those people were greatly indebted to their personal strength. The cause of this was, that they were, in a high degree, deficient in the improvements of art, especially in their knowledge and command of the mechanical powers. Their chief substitute for this want was their own bodily powers. It was incumbent on them, therefore, to increase those powers in the highest practicable degree. The invention of gunpowder has brought the weak and the strong to an equality in war; and the improvements made in mechanics have done nearly the same in relation to the arts of peace. Hence, as respects the general business of life, the moderns have much less necessity for personal strength than the ancients had. And, as mankind act from motives of necessity and interest much more than from those of any other sort, physical education, the chief source of superior strength of person, has been greatly neglected, especially by the higher orders of society, for two or three centuries. Knowledge being now the only ground of great power and influence, *intellectual education* receives at present a much more *exclusive* attention than it formerly did, and much more than comports with the benefit of our race. Even *it*, however, would profit greatly by an improved condition of physical education.

This brings me immediately to my task. But before actually entering on it, suffer me to observe, that if, instead of treating technically of moral, intellectual, and physical education, authors and others would speak correctly of the education of the different portions of the body, each portion being trained according to its organization and character, they would be more philosophical and intelligible than they are. I am persuaded they would be also more instructive.

The skin, for example, must be educated by one mode of discipline, the stomach by another, the lungs by a third, the muscles and circulatory system by a fourth, and each external sense and cerebral organ by a method corresponding to the peculiarity of its nature. In this view of the subject, which is the only rational one, the training of the brain in all its departments, by whatever name they may be called, is as truly a *physical* or *physiological* process as the training of any other part of the body. I shall not, however, out of mere conformity to these principles, employ at present any new terms or phrases, as those already in use are sufficient for my purpose, and will be better understood than such as I might substitute for them. It is of physical education, then, in the usual acceptation of the phrase, that I am now to speak.

This process may be defined, *that scheme of training which contributes most effectually to the development, health, and perfection of living matter.* As applied to man, it is that scheme which raises his whole system to its summit of perfection. In this are included the highest tone and vigour of all parts of the body, that are consistent with a sound condition of them; for the tone of a vital organ, like that of a musical instrument, may be too high, as well as too low.

Physical education, then, in its philosophy and practice, is of great compass. If complete, it would be tantamount to an entire system of Hygeiene. It would embrace every thing that, by bearing in any way on the human body, might injure or benefit it in its health, vigour, and fitness for action. It must be obvious to you, therefore, that, on the present occasion, I can consider it but partially. To give a full development of it, volumes of writing would be necessary, and days would be required to read them. So numerous are the elements which enter into the aggregate of the scheme, that I can but barely refer to most of them, and speak of a few of them very briefly.

Were I to commence at the real fountain of physical education, and trace the stream to its close, I should be obliged to refer to a period anterior to the birth or even the formation of those, of the promotion and perfection of whose health and strength I should be treating.

The first and most important element of physical education is to procure, for those to be educated, a *constitution of body originally sound*. To this the soundness of parents is indispensable—it being a law of nature that constitutional qualities are hereditary. As relates to leading points, this is a truism familiar to every one, and is uniformly and successfully acted on in the breeding of inferior animals. That all constitutional qualities are transmitted from parents to their children, admits not of a doubt. Apparent exceptions are only apparent, not real. Are parents perfectly sound and vigorous in body? So are their children, when they first see the light. Is the reverse true? Are the former constitutionally unsound and debilitated? The evil descends, in some degree, to the latter. Respecting intellect, the same is true. According as it is weak or strong, sound, unsound, or peculiar in the parents, so are its character and condition in the children. I speak in general terms, and refer only to general results, without meaning to entangle myself in the difficulties of abnormal cases. And thus far all testimony concurs to sustain me. The descendants of a community, sound, vigorous, and hardy in mind and body, will be themselves a community of the same description, unless they are changed by adventitious causes. To this, neither does history contain, no can observation adduce, a single exception. Spartan children were like their Spartan parents, and Bœotian children like their Bœotian parents. And, in our times, the descendants of the hill-country and of the valley are very dissimilar.

As relates to the standing and welfare of the human race, this principle is much more extensively and powerfully operative than it is generally supposed to be. It is the reason why children born at different periods of the lives of their parents, and under the influence of different circumstances, especially different degrees of parental health and vigour, are often so unlike each other. It is also the most probable source of the very frequent and strong resemblance of twins, which receive the impress of exactly the same parental condition. Children partake of the constitutional qualities of their parents for the time being. Years and circumstances alter those qualities, and the offspring produced under the influence of them thus modified, are correspondingly altered. Even the present predominance of any particular faculty of the mind in the parents, would seem to transmit that faculty to the child in greater vigour than it would be transmitted under the predominance of any other faculty. To illustrate this subject by examples.

The first-born children of parents who marry when very young, are rarely, if ever, equal, in either body or intellect, to those born at a subsequent period, provided the parents continue healthy. Hence the younger sons of noblemen so generally surpass, in all the higher attributes of our race, their elder brothers, whose only pre-eminence depends on the privileges attached to primogeniture. I know that an attempt has been made to explain this on a different ground; that of education, expectancy, and habit. But I also know that the attempt has failed. The difference is too great to be thus accounted for. It often occurs, moreover, when the cause just referred to is wanting. The following is believed to be the true explanation.

Very young parents are, in constitution, immature and

comparatively feeble; and that constitutional imperfection descends to their early offspring. As years pass on, their being ripens, and their strength increases. As a natural effect of this, the constitutions of their children become ameliorated. It was a knowledge of this, derived from observation, that induced the Spartans to prohibit marriage until the parties had attained entire maturity; the females the age of twenty-two or twenty-five, and the males that of twenty-seven or thirty. I need scarcely add, that they were personally the hardiest and most powerful people of Greece, and, as a community, the most warlike.

For reasons well known to phrenologists, the animal organs and faculties predominate during early life. Parents, therefore, who marry at that period, communicate in a higher degree to their first children the same unfortunate predominance, which renders them less intellectual and moral, and more sensual; less capable, as well as less ambitious, of pre-eminence in knowledge and virtue, and more inclined to animal indulgences. If I am not mistaken, history and observation sustain this view of the subject, and philosophy expounds it.

Again. The sons of soldiers and military leaders, born during periods of war and peril, are believed to be constitutionally brave. Under such circumstances, a coward has rarely been issued into the world. The reason would seem plain. In the parents, the organs and faculties pertaining to war, excited to inordinate action by scenes congenial to them, predominate for the time, and bravery becomes the native inheritance of their sons. Hence also the phrase " soldier's daughter" means a heroic woman. During the early and warlike age of our frontier States, when the rifle and the tommahock were constantly employed in the work of havock, every child was born an Indian-fighter. The cause, I say, is obvious. In the whole population, which was composed of warriors, the organs and faculties suited to the occasion bore sway, and gave to the constitution of the offspring of the community a corresponding character. For the same reason children born in France during the revolution, were constitutionally soldiers. The late spectacle of heroism in Paris testifies strongly to this effect. Those who defeated the veterans of Charles X., and wrested from him the sceptre and the sword, were chiefly the sons of the preceding revolution. And never did combatants display valour more firm and resplendent.*

Efforts are again made to explain these and all similar events, on the single ground of education and example. But they are made in vain: or rather worse than in vain. They inculcate error. That education and example do much, is not denied. And the principles of their operation will be stated hereafter. But they cannot do every thing. Children born under the shade of the laurel become brave soldiers and heroic leaders more readily than those who inhale, with their first breath, the perfume of the olive. This is in accordance with nature; and observation, as far as it has been directed to the subject, testifies to its truth. It is on similar ground that the superior bravery of the Spartans and Lacedemonians may be most rationally explained. I mean the active predominance of the warlike organs in their parents.

On the same principle are we to explain the fact, that the children of Arabs and Tartars are born with propensities to pillage and theft. For centuries, their progenitors have been a pilfering and a " robber race." The consequence is obvious. The organs of the brain inclining to those vices have been predominant. They have formed the constitutional bias and ruling passion of their possessors, and have, no doubt, been enlarged by perpetual exercise; for exercise as certainly enlarges

* The subject here touched upon by Dr Caldwell—the transmission to the child of the qualities predominant in the parents at the time of its production—is one of very great importance, though hitherto almost universally overlooked. Professor Hufeland of Berlin, in his *Art of Prolonging Human Life*, insists upon it with earnestness (see English translation, London, 1829, pp. 214, 215); and it is largely illustrated by Mr Combe in the fifth chapter of his work on *The Constitution of Man considered in relation to External Objects.*—R. C.

particular portions of the brain, as it does particular muscles. By a law of nature, therefore, their excess in both size and action has descended to posterity; and this excess has been augmented by example and practice. The Arab and Tartar character, therefore, is the product of the combined influence of parentage and education.

The first suggestion I shall offer, as a means toward the improvement of our race, is the prohibition or voluntary abandonment of too early marriages. Before the parties form a compact fraught with consequences so infinitely weighty, let the constitution and education of both be matured. They will then not only transmit to their offspring a better organization, but be themselves, from the knowledge and experience they have attained, better prepared to improve it by cultivation. For I shall endeavour to make it appear that cultivation can improve it. When a skilful agriculturist wishes to amend his breed of cattle, he does not employ, for that purpose, immature animals. On the contrary, he carefully prevents their intercourse. Experience, moreover, teaches him not to expect fruit of the best quality from immature fruit-trees or vines. The product of such crudeness is always defective. In like manner, marriages between boarding-school girls and striplings in or just out of college, ought to be prohibited. In such cases, prohibition is a duty, no less to the parties themselves, than to their offspring and society. Marriages of the kind are rarely productive of any thing desirable. Mischief and unhappiness of some sort are their natural fruit. Patriotism, therefore, philanthropy, and every feeling of kindness to human nature, call for their prevention. Objections, resting on ground not altogether dissimilar, may be justly urged against young women marrying men far advanced in years. Old men should in no case contract marriages likely to prove fruitful. Age has impaired their constitutional qualities, which descending to their offspring, the practice tends to deteriorate our race. It is rare for the descendants of men far advanced in years to be distinguished for high qualities of either body or mind.

As respects persons seriously deformed, or in any way constitutionally enfeebled—the rickety and club-footed, for instance, and those with distorted spines, or who are predisposed to insanity, scrofula, pulmonary consumption, gout, or epilepsy—all persons of this description should conscientiously abstain from matrimony. In a special manner, where both the male and female labour under a hereditary taint, they should make it a part of their duty to God and their posterity never to be thus united. Marriage in such individuals cannot be defended on moral ground, much less on that of public usefulness. It is selfish to an extent but little short of crime. Its abandonment or prevention would tend, in a high degree, to the improvement of mankind.

As relates to the present, in common with all other subjects, facts alone are worthy of our attention. A single one, that may be here adduced, is preferable to all the theories that can be framed. It confirms so fully the principle I am contending for, as to render opposition to it hopeless.

In Turkey and Persia, men of rank and wealth marry none but well formed and beautiful women. They procure many of their wives from Georgia and Circassia, the Asiatic paradise of female beauty. Such has been their practice for ages. The consequence is what all enlightened individuals are prepared to expect. As regards their *persons*, the Turks and Persians of the higher casts are among the finest people on earth. Compared to the lower orders of their countrymen, who marry without such selection, and for whose personal improvement, therefore, no provision is made, their superiority, in all points of elegance, is as striking as is that of the English hunter contrasted with the cart-horse. Throughout the world, a similar custom would produce a similar effect. It is to be lamented, however, that the practice in Turkey and Persia, of so secluding females as to prevent them from using the proper amount of exercise, operates as a barrier to the improvement of mankind. I need scarcely add, that it does this by debilitating the female constitution, and entailing comparative feebleness on the offspring. Let it be borne in mind, that, in speaking of the fine forms of the Turks and Persians, I allude to their " persons" only, by which I mean their limbs and trunks. In the development and figure of their heads, they are inferior to the Europeans and the inhabitants of the United States. The reason is plain. Being less devoted to intellectual pursuits, their brains experience less excitement and exercise, and are therefore smaller, and probably also inferior in tone.

To illustrate this subject farther, and fortify the sentiments just advanced, the citation of another practice of skilful agriculturists may be useful. It is that of selecting the largest, best formed, and sprightliest of their domestic animals as breeders, when they wish to improve their stock. The same is true of their efforts to improve even their vegetable productions. Whether they propagate by seeds, roots, or cuttings, they select the largest, best looking, and best conditioned, as the parent race. This practice is founded on experience, and the end aimed at by it, except it be prevented by sinister causes, is always attained. Its relevancy to the subject I am considering is too plain to need any comment. The practice of Frederick II. of Prussia, on this point, is well known. He was inordinately attached to a gigantic stature in his grenadiers. To form this corps, therefore, he selected the largest men in his kingdom. Nor did his solicitude on the subject suffer him to stop here. That the race might not degenerate, he also selected, as wives for his grenadiers, the largest women in his kingdom. The consequence is, that Potsdam and its neighbourhood, where Frederick's grenadier-corps was stationed, furnish even now a greater number of persons of gigantic size, than any other place of the same amount of population in Europe—perhaps in the world.

In consequence of an unfortunate cerebral organization, some persons who are reared in virtuous society, under the influence of the best example, possess an incontrollable propensity to vice—to lying, treachery, theft, robbery, and even murder. Instances of this description are much more numerous than they are thought to be. In case of the marriage of such individuals, the probability is strong that their offspring will inherit their constitutional infirmity. The issue, indeed, can scarcely be otherwise, unless it be prevented by a better organization in the other parent, or counteracted by education, of whose influence in amending mankind I shall speak hereafter. To refrain from marriage, therefore, would be, in those persons, a redeeming virtue. Of individuals dwarfish in stature, the same is true. All such acts of self-denial would be praiseworthy in them, inasmuch as they would tend to ameliorate the condition of man.

Another source of human deterioration is a long series of family intermarriages. Be the *cause* what it may, both history and observation testify to the *fact*, that the issue of marriages between parties related by consanguinity always degenerate. They become enfeebled in time, both mentally and corporeally. This practice, which is fostered chiefly by the false pride of rank, has reduced almost to dwarfishness the nobility of several nations, especially of Portugal. It has likewise aided not a little in not only deteriorating, but nearly extinguishing, most of the royal families of Europe. This case is strengthened and rendered more impressive by the fact, that the ancestors of those families were the real *proceres* or *natural nobles* of the land; men peculiarly distinguished in their day, as well for corporeal stature, strength, and comeliness, as for mental excellence. Yet, I repeat, that a long line of family intermarriages has contributed much to reduce below the average of mankind the descendants of those ancient nobles, whose high qualities alone gave them station and influence. In this the human race are analogous to our domestic animals, which are deteriorated by breeding constantly from the same stock. Even among the people of certain sects in religion, much mischief is done by the continued intermarriages of the members with each other. The condition of the Jews and the Quakers affords proof of this. Those two societies are more afflicted with some form of mental derangement, in proportion to their numbers, than any others in Christendom. They are also unusually deficient in distinguished men. This is no doubt attributable, in no small degree, to their so seldom marrying out of their own sects.

Another grand source of the degeneracy of human beings, is the marriage of the indigent; of those, I mean, who are destitute of a competent supply of wholesome food for themselves and their children. This is a fearful cause of deterioration. Reason assures us that it must be so. A sound and powerful machine cannot be constructed out of a scanty stock of damaged materials. And to the decision of reason, observation unites its tesimony. A glance at the indigent of all nations furnishes incontestable proof of the fact. Monuments of far-gone degeneracy every where present themselves. Witness the large manufacturing towns of Europe. Stinted and unwholesome fare acts on mankind as it does on other forms of living matter. It injures organization, and checks development. Both the vegetables of a barren soil, and the animals scantily nourished by them, are diminutive and feeble, as well as unsightly. So is man, when pinched and dispirited by poverty and its concomitants. Even the United States furnish many examples confirmatory of this, while other countries furnish a hundred-fold more. Such are a few of the most prominent and fruitful sources of human degeneracy. The remedy for the evil is, abstinence from marriage in the cases referred to.

But in no country, perhaps, and least of all in our own, are we to look for the speedy adoption, to any useful extent, of this preventive measure. People will marry and have issue, whether their figures and developments be good or bad, whether they are poor or rich, akin or aliens in blood, and whether their constitutions be sound or otherwise. They will also continue to marry, in many instances, at too early a period of life, as long as subsistence for a family can be easily procured. Our only practicable remedy, therefore, consists in removing, as far as possible, the evils of improper parentage and other causes, by subsequent treatment. And this can be done by education alone, judiciously adapted, in its principles and administration, to the constitution of man.

The last cause I shall cite, as operating before the birth of the child, is the state of health of the mother during gestation. Unless that be sound, the constitution of the offspring will be necessarily impaired. It is in vain to allege, in opposition to this, that the infants of delicate, enfeebled, and even sickly mothers, are sometimes healthy and robust. They would have been more so, had the health of their mothers been in a better condition.

The avoidance, by females, therefore, while pregnant, of every thing that might injure them, cannot be too strict. Nor is this all. They should take more exercise in the open air than they usually do. The feeling which induces many of them to shut themselves up in their rooms for weeks and months before parturition is an excess of delicacy—were the term less exceptionable, I would say false delicacy—and ought not to be indulged. Their food should be wholesome, nourishing, and easy of digestion, and should be taken in quantities sufficient to give them their entire strength, and maintain all their functions in full vigour. Their minds ought to be kept in a state of tranquillity. In a particular manner, the effects of frightful appearances, alarming accidents, and agitating and impassioned tales and narratives should be carefully guarded against by them. The blighting operation of the "Reign of Terror," in Paris, on the children born during that period, furnishes fearful evidence of the influence of the distracted and horrified condition of the mother over the system of the unborn infant. An unusual number of them was still-born. Of those who were not so, a number equally uncommon died at an early age; and of those who attained adult life, an unusual proportion were subject to epilepsy, madness, or some other form of cerebral disease. Pinel tells us, that out of ninety-two children born after the blowing up of the arsenal at Landau, in 1793, eight were affected by a species of cretinism, and died before the expiration of the fifth year; thirty-three languished through a miserable existence of from nine to ten months' duration; sixteen died on coming into the world, and two were born with *numerous fractures* of the longer bones! The latter effect must have been produced by the inordinate and deranged contraction of the uterus.

Over the foregoing causes, you, as mere instructors, have no control. For no mismanagement of them, therefore, are you accountable. Nor does the direction of physical education in the nursery fall within your province. Yet is the treatment of children there of great moment, both to them and to you, in subsequent years. Its effects, for good or evil, can scarcely fail to be as lasting as their lives, and to influence more or less their entire destiny. A few remarks on it, therefore, will not, perhaps, be out of place.

The sound nursery-education of children consists chiefly in the judicious management of diet, cleanliness, clothing, atmospherical temperature, respiration, muscular exercise, sleep, and the *animal* passions. I say " animal passions," because children in the nursery have no other kind. Of the education of the moral feelings, I shall speak hereafter. I do not say that no degree of moral education can be communicated to children at a very early period. Their moral organs, however, being as yet not only small, but very immature, cannot be operated on to much advantage. An attempt to excite them powerfully might even do mischief.

Diet.—For many reasons, infants are best nourished when nursed by their mothers. Though exceptions to this sometimes occur, they are rare, and might, by well-regulated conduct, be rendered much more so. When children have passed the period of lactation, their diet should be simple, nutritious, and easily digested; and they may take it liberally, and at shorter intervals than adults. But they should never be gorged with it, nor allowed to eat until their appetites are cloyed. Of all solid substances, whether animal or vegetable, they should early learn the importance of *thorough mastication*. They should be taught, that to swallow such articles without chewing them is indecent, as well as injurious; for they will often do, in defiance of danger and positive prohibition, what they would not do in violation of good manners. High-seasoned condiments, and other provocatives, should be carefully withheld from them. So should unripe fruit, and crude vegetables,—all their diet being thoroughly cooked. Indeed, children are, on an average, much more injured than benefited by eating undressed summer fruit, of whatever kind it may be, and whether it be ripe or green. One reason of this is, that they are permitted to eat too much of it, and to take it at improper times. Every thing either highly stimulating, or difficult of digestion, should be prohibited food. Such diet is bad enough for adults; for children, tender, feeble, and susceptible as they are, it is poison, destroying life, at times, in a few hours. Infinite mischief is done by giving children a "*little*" of a prohibited article, because "the dear creatures wanted it, and held out their little hands for it!" A transgression of this kind by a nurse should be visited on her by an immediate dismissal. Let it never be forgotten or overlooked, that, like all other parts of the body, the stomach may be strengthened by skilful training. Let that organ receive suitable aliment, in proper quantities, and at well-regulated periods, and it will be as certainly improved in its powers and sympathies, as the brain, external senses, and muscles are, by their appropriate kinds of action. Nor is it less impaired and enfeebled than other organs, by too much or too little action. It is subject to all the laws that govern other portions of organized matter. Suitable exercise, indulged in to the proper extent, strengthens it, while excessive and deficient action weakens it, and unfits it for its functions. Too much attention cannot be paid to the bowels, in the earlier years of life, and indeed throughout the whole of it. Their condition should always be free, inclining to laxity rather than the contrary. Let them be regulated by diet and regimen, if possible. Should that course, however, prove unsuccessful, the necessary laxatives must be administered.

The *cleanliness* of children is indispensable to the healthy action of their skin, and, through that, to their general health; and the water used in cleansing them should be tepid. Though vigorous children may bear bathing in cold water with impunity, delicate ones cannot; and even the former, if in the slightest degree indisposed, may be injured by it. It being, moreover, not always easy to ascertain whether children are in perfect health or not, tepid water is always safest. Nor is infancy the proper period to attempt to produce hardihood of constitution, by exposure to a low temperature. Practice founded on the opposite opinion is often productive of serious, not to say fatal, results.

I shall only add, under this head, that personal cleanliness, as one of the minor virtues (for it deserves to be so called), is much less attended to and esteemed in the United States than it ought to be. Nor does this charge implicate only the neglect of children. Adults are still more negligent of cleanliness in themselves. During weeks and months, water touches no parts of many of them, save their hands and faces, and, *longo intervallo*, their feet and ancles. This is downright *uncleanliness*, not to give it a harsher name. Were the inhabitants of our country to use some form of ablution much more frequently than they do, they would be purer, more comfortable, and healthier than they are.*

---

* Were the philosophy of cleanliness better known, this duty would not be so generally neglected. The skin has innumerable pores, and serves as an outlet for the waste particles of the body. The quantity of noxious matter excreted through these pores in twenty-four hours is, on the very lowest estimate, about twenty-four ounces. If the passage of this matter be obstructed, so that it is retained in the body, the quality of the blood is deteriorated by its presence, and the general health, which greatly depends on the state of the blood, is made to suffer. The nature of the perspired matter is such, that it is apt, in consequence of the evaporation of its watery portion, to be condensed, and clog the

The *clothing* of infants should be soft, fitted to absorb moisture from the skin and retain the natural warmth of the body, and so fashioned as to be loose and free. The tight bandaging of children, and every other form of pressure made by their clothing, is pernicious. Health has been injured, and life destroyed by it. This is true, more especially, of undue pressure on the abdomen or chest—the parts on which it is most frequently made.

The *temperature* of a nursery ought to be comfortable. It should neither chill with cold nor flush with heat. To the tenderness and susceptibility of infancy, all extremes are hurtful. Means to prevent the apartment from being traversed by currents of cold or damp air should be provided, and nothing neglected that may tend to secure an equable temperature.

The *respiration* of infants is immensely important, and cannot be too vigilantly attended to. The air breathed

---

pores of the skin; and hence the necessity for washing the surface frequently, so as to keep the pores open, and allow perspiration to be freely performed. The clothing, moreover, must be so porous and clean as readily to absorb and allow a passage to the matter perspired, otherwise the same result ensues as from impurity of the skin, namely the obstruction of the process of perspiration. Nor is this all. The skin is an absorbing as well as an excreting organ, foreign substances in contact with it being sucked into its pores and introduced into the blood. Hence, when cleanliness is neglected, the evil consequence is twofold: 1*st*, The pores, as we have seen, are clogged, and the perspiration obstructed; and, 2*dly*, Part of the noxious matter on the skin or clothing is absorbed into the system, where it produces hurtful effects. From an exposition of the structure and functions of the skin, therefore, the necessity for cleanliness of person and clothing becomes abundantly evident; and the corresponding *duty* of cleanliness is more likely to be performed by persons who know what has just been stated, than by those who are impelled to performance by injunctions alone. In some parts of the East, ablution of the body is justly regarded as a religious duty; but it needs not to be told how extensively this duty is neglected in Britain. When men become enlightened, a warm bath, once a-week at least, will be considered one of the necessaries of life:— those who are in the habit of keeping their skin in a proper condition, by means of bathing and friction, will bear testimony to the increase of comfort and activity which is thus secured.—R. C.

by them should be fresh and pure. Let nurseries, therefore, be spacious, clean, and thoroughly ventilated. Nor is it unimportant that they be *well lighted*—I mean with windows. The influence of light on animal life is not sufficiently appreciated. Facts as well as principles shew, that it is much greater and more salutary than is commonly believed. Darkness, long continued, is scarcely less pernicious to tender animals (and children are such) than to plants. Account for it as we may, light co-operates with oxygen, in imparting to the arterial blood the brilliancy of its scarlet. Not only the complexion, but the blood itself, the source of complexion, loses much of its florid hue, in miners, criminals confined in dark dungeons, and other persons long secluded from the light. During suitable weather, infants should pass several hours daily in the open air. The constant housing of adults is bad; that of infants far worse—because their delicacy and sensitiveness are greater. Respiration acts primitively on the lungs; and those organs are invigorated and otherwise benefited, by the laughing, shouting, crowing, and occasional *crying* of children. However unpleasant the latter sound may be, it is a natural one. And nature is, in all things, our best guide; though we must not abuse her, or suffer her to be abused, by any sort of excess. Crying, within proper bounds, is *good exercise* for the lungs and other vocal organs of children; and suitable exercise is a certain source of strength to every portion of the body. The late Professor Rush, who was noted for his pithy, antithetical, and sagacious remarks, said in his lectures, that, though the usual adage respecting children was, " Laugh and be fat," he had learned from observation that they might also " cry and be fat." And he was right.*

* The qualification " within proper bounds" is judicious; for excess in crying is unquestionably hurtful. Dr John Gregory remarks, that " children, when very young, never cry but from pain or sickness, and therefore the cause of their distress should be accurately inquired into. If it is allowed to continue, it disturbs all the animal functions, especially the digestive powers; and from the disorders of these most

The *muscular exercise* of children should be regulated with more judgment and care than are usually bestowed on it. Crawling is their first mode of progression. In this they should be encouraged, and induced to practise it freely; and it ought to be somewhat protracted. Nurses and parents, especially young parents, are generally too anxious to see their infants beginning to walk, or rather to totter along in a form of movement that can hardly be called walking. Hence they induce them to make premature efforts to that effect. The evils likely to arise, and which often do arise, from this practice, are plain. Owing to the immaturity and flexibility of their bones, and the feebleness of their muscles, the lower extremities are frequently bent and misshapen by it; and the children, falling, injure their heads or other parts of their bodies, by bringing them into collision with hard, cutting, or puncturing substances. The precise age at which children may begin to walk with safety cannot be settled by any general rule. The progress toward maturity being more rapid in some of them than in others, the periods of their fitness to walk will be earlier or later in corresponding degrees. But none should be allowed to walk until the firmness and strength of their limbs are sufficient to sustain, without distortion or injury, the weight of their bodies. Observation on individual cases, therefore, aided by experience, must give the rule. On

of children's diseases proceed. The cries of a child are the voice of nature supplicating relief. It can express its wants by no other language. Instead of hearkening to this voice, we often stifle it by putting the little wretch in a cradle, where the noise and violent motion confounds all its senses, and extinguishes all feelings of pain in a forced and unnatural sleep. Sometimes they are allowed to cry till their strength is exhausted. Their violent struggles to get relief, and the agitations of their passions, equally disorder their constitutions; and when a child's first sensations partake so much of pain and distress, and when the turbulent passions are so early awakened and exercised, there is reason to suspect they may have too great an influence on the future temper." (*Comparative View of the State and Faculties of Man with those of the Animal World*, 3d edit. p. 40.)—R. C.

the subject of sleep, as a means in physical education, a few remarks will be offered hereafter.

The *passions* of children, if indulged, are growing evils. Hence they should be vigilantly held in check from the earliest period. If not thus restrained, they become noxious weeds in the garden of the mind, deprive valuable plants of their nourishment, and blight them with their shadow. To speak in language better suited to my subject; if, instead of being curbed, they are fed and fostered, they become the ruling elements of character, and insure to the individual a life of trouble— not to say of accident, disease, and suffering. A large proportion of the evils of life, as respects both health and fortune, is the product, more or less directly, of unruly passions. The higher and milder virtues, social as well as moral, cannot flourish under their dominion. In a special manner, children should never be allowed to obtain what has once been denied them, by breaking into a passion about it. Such an act ought to be always visited by a positive privation of the thing desired; and the ground of the denial should be made known to them. Never let a child have reason to believe that a gust of passion is a suitable means to gratify a wish. Teach him, as far as possible, to know and feel the reverse; and, should he become offended at a pet or a play-thing, neither beat it yourself, nor allow him to beat it, by way of pacification or revenge. Such procedure is aliment to vindictiveness, and leads to mischief—perhaps, in the end, to maiming and murder. As relates to matters of this kind, ignorant and passionate nurses are among the worst of family nuisances. They often blow into a flame the sparks of passion, which, without their aid, would have slumbered and gone out. These may be deemed small and trivial matters. In themselves they are so, but not in their consequences. Let it never be forgotten, that " little things are great to little men," and more especially to little children. A fiery education in the nursery may heat the brain to the verge of inflammation, and aid in the production of actual inflammation or madness,—impair health in sundry other ways by excessive excitement,—render unhappy the days of others, as well as of the mismanaged individual,—and lay the foundation of a blasted reputation. It is believed that an education of this kind injured immeasurably the late Lord Byron; and Earl Ferrers expiated on a gibbet the fruit of a similar one.

But it is not what is called the *temper* that is alone injured by a nursery-education unskilfully conducted. Habits of deception, falsehood, and even theft, are not unfrequently encouraged and formed by it. This can scarcely fail to lead to serious mischief; it being the natural course of things, that seeds sown in infancy yield fruit in maturer years. The slightest disposition, therefore, in children to deviate from truth and candour, either in words or actions, or to appropriate as their own what does not belong to them, should be promptly suppressed. It arises from irregular action in certain organs of the brain, which, if not checked, runs to excess, and turns to a moral disease. The organs referred to belong to the animal class, and, being thus exercised, become so powerful and refractory as to be no longer under the control of the moral and reflecting organs; and the elements of vice are finally rooted in the constitution with such firmness as to frustrate all attempts to remove them. So important is early training to the character of our race, yet so lamentably is it neglected and abused! In such cases, health of body suffers in common with soundness of mind, the undue exercise of the animal organs of the brain being hostile to both. In fine, the regulation of the nursery, though too generally intrusted to ignorance and thoughtlessness, is a charge of great importance, imposing a responsibility far more weighty than it is usually considered.* Too often are those who are fit for little else converted into nursery-girls. It may be safely as-

* There is nothing in which philosophical writers on education are more unanimous, than in holding that the training bestowed on infants in the earliest years, is by far the most important in reference to their future character. " The great mistake," says Locke, " I have observed

serted, that the charge of the nursery is frequently given to those who would not be trusted with the care of the sheepfold. This is unpardonable, and leads to evil by a law as certain and immutable, as that by which warmth and moisture excite vegetation, or a ponderous body inclines towards the centre.

But if the mere neglect of parents is a sure source of vice in their children, and therefore highly blameable,

in people's breeding their children has been, that this has not been taken care enough of in its due season; that the mind has not been made obedient to discipline, and pliant to reason, when at first it was most tender, most easy to be bowed."—(*Some Thoughts concerning Education*, § 34.) Montaigne says: "Plato reprehending a boy for playing at some childish game, 'Thou reprovest me,' says the boy, 'for a very little thing:' 'Custom,' replied Plato, 'is no little thing.' And he was right; for I find that our greatest vices derive their first propensity from our most tender infancy, and that our principal education depends upon the nurse."—(*Essays*, b. i. chap. 22.) "Practical education," says Miss Edgeworth, "begins very early, even in the nursery... The temper acquires habits much earlier than is usually apprehended; the first impressions which infants receive, and the first habits which they learn from their nurses, influence the temper and disposition, long after the slight causes which produced them are forgotten."—(*Practical Education*, vol. i. p. 12.) And Mr Mill, in the article "Education," *Encyc. Brit.*, observes: "It seems to be a law of human nature that the first sensations experienced produce the greatest effects...Common language confirms this law, when it speaks of the susceptibility of the tender mind...Education, then, or the care of forming the habits, ought to commence as much as possible with the period of sensation itself; and at no period is its utmost vigilance of greater importance than at first." The credulity of young children, and the firm hold which earliest opinions take upon the mind, are of themselves sufficiently strong reasons for dispensing with the services of those ignorant nursery-maids, who implant so many hurtful errors and prejudices which it is almost impossible to eradicate. "For," as Jeremy Taylor forcibly remarks, "whatsoever is taught to children at first they believe infinitely, for they know nothing to the contrary; they have had no other masters whose theorems might abate the strength of their first persuasions; and it is a great advantage in those cases to get possession; and before their first principles can be dislodged, they are made habitual and complexional—it is their nature then to believe them." (*Discourse of the Liberty of Prophesying*, sect. xi. § 4.)—R. C.

where can I find terms to reprobate, as it deserves, the criminality of corrupt and profligate parental examples! or how sufficiently to deplore the disasters they entail on families and the community! To pronounce them, by way of distinction in guilt and mischief, THE CURSE OF THE LAND, would not be a denunciation too deep for their demerits. For when I calmly reflect on their inherent turpitude, and survey the whole scope of their influence, direct and indirect, present and future, I am compelled to regard them as a fountain of evil more hateful and prolific than any other. Contrasted with them, the seductive influence of youthful associates whitens into innocence. If guilt and infamy are a greater evil, and more to be deprecated than disease and death, there might be difficulty in proving to the satisfaction of sound reason, that parental infanticide is a deeper crime than parental profligacy. The former but consigns to the grave a single innocent, saving it from the ills that humanity must endure; while the latter is instrumental in rendering a whole family monuments of depravity, vice, and misery, revolting to sense, outcasts from affection and sympathy, and, as far as their influence extends, a blight on society. Nor does the evil terminate with themselves. They in turn become profligate parents and infect their descendants; and thus the stream of corruption runs on and widens, diffusing its mildews to an unknown extent. I repeat, that if destruction of mind is worse in all respects than destruction of body (and who will deny it?) I can scarcely perceive on what ground the deliberate perpetrator of the former deed should be held less criminal, than he who under a gust of impassioned excitement perpetrates the latter. Besides, the profligacy of parental example not only brutalizes the *minds* of children; it leads also to bodily diseases in them, which hurry them as lazars to premature graves. And thus to the infectious example of the parent is the death of the children virtually attributable.

Will it be alleged that I am delineating too broadly and colouring too highly this picture of family immorality and its consequences? I reply, that I do not think so; and instances innumerable in proof of my opinion might be easily cited. There is scarcely in the United States a village or a neighbourhood that does not furnish them, and towns and cities exhibit them in thousands. Or will it be alleged that parents are not aware of the full extent of the desolation they spread around them by their pestilent example? I again reply, that it is not possible for them to be ignorant of facts which they daily witness; and which, had not habitual vice and profligacy hardened their consciences, would madden them with remorse. Does vegetation wither under the emanations of the mancinella and the upas? and does poison bred of *material* corruption infect and destroy the most powerful frames? We know it does. How, then, can the tender and susceptible minds of childhood and youth resist the poison of *moral* corruption? especially when it is administered by a parent, on whom the child has been accustomed to rely for mental as well as corporeal sustenance. Under such circumstances, to escape contamination is all but impossible. If the infection does not strike in one form, it will in another. Of this the parent must be sensible, because he sees it. He therefore sins deliberately against knowledge, and is not only a felonious, but an unnatural destroyer.

Tell not me that any man believes he can rear a family in virtue, industry, and usefulness, or that any human means can save them from vice and pollution, while he is himself an idler or a spendthrift, a gambler or a debauchee, a drunkard, a profane swearer, a brawler, a liar and a slanderer, or an open cheat; or while he indulges in impure and licentious conversation, or destroys the peace and harmony of his fire-side by habitual outbreakings of groundless jealousy, unprovoked rage, or any other form of furious passion. And, if these outrages on morals, or any of them, be indulged in by a mother, I need hardly say that the scene is still more revolting, and, in some respects, the catastrophe more deplorable. When the palm and the olive shall spring up and be fruitful on the rocks of Spitzbergen, and in other respects the present laws of nature shall give place to new ones, then, and not before, may filial morality flourish under the bane of parental profligacy.

Morality, in brief, is the growth of home, early impressions, virtuous example, and *practical* lessons, as essentially as the pomegranate and the banana are the growth of regions bordering on the sun. I do not deny that the reading and studying of moral productions, especially the biographical memoirs of virtuous and distinguished characters, and an attendance on moral exhortations in academies, colleges, places of public worship, and elsewhere, are useful. Far from it. But I contend that their influence is limited; that they make but a small portion of the aggregate that constitutes a complete moral education; and that a reliance far too exclusive is placed on them, to the neglect of means that are much more effectual. And I further contend, that parents, especially *mothers*, whose responsibility to God and society for the conduct of their children is unspeakably weighty—I contend that they have it in their power to do for the morality of the country ten thousand-fold more than all our teachers of theology, literature, and science, and all our pastors of churches united. By reading, and an attendance on public instruction, much may be learnt of the science of morals. But habits of correct and efficient morality, and a fruitful love and pursuit of virtue, are the issue chiefly of practice and example under the parental roof. Never, until views like these have been adopted as rules of action, will man possess the moral soundness of which he is susceptible.

The *teething* of children, is a process requiring some attention. Provided, however, health be otherwise maintained, it is much less dangerous than it is usually considered. The only reason why the young of the human race do not cut their teeth with as little difficulty and suffering as those of the inferior animals is, because they are rendered, by the treatment they receive, especially by improprieties in diet, unnaturally tender and sensitive.

Gastric and constitutional derangement is the chief cause, not only why infants do not cut their teeth with ease and without sickness, but also why they suffer so much from diseases of them in after life. More attention to general health than is now paid, not alone during infantile and youthful, but likewise during adult age, even to the close of life, would greatly limit the business of the dentist. To the cleanliness of the teeth and gums of children, strict attention should be paid.

It needs scarcely be observed, that, as a preventive of smallpox, children should be vaccinated at an early age. The practice, therefore, may be regarded as an important element of nursery education. The neglect or improper procrastination of it, devolves on parents a responsibility as weighty as almost any other respecting infants, of which they can be guilty.

As already mentioned, however, these things affect you, as teachers, but remotely; yet they *do* affect you—because your profession calls you to witness their products, and to remedy, as far as possible, the mischief they have done. The pupil of the *nursery* carries, as the fruit of his tuition there, a given character into your schools. And that character accords with his previous training. I doubt not that many of you have learned to read and decipher, in children, a correct record, and one not easily mistaken or forgotten, of the family government of their parents. Were fathers and mothers apprized of the fact, that their offspring are correct informants, at the bar of the public, of what they daily see, and hear, and experience at home, a sense of reputation alone, in the absence of higher motives, would induce them to amend their domestic discipline. Such at least ought to be its effect. Children trained to obedience and attention in their own dwellings, will not, when they enter seats of instruction, leave those valuable qualities behind them. But if they are neglected by their parents, they can scarcely fail to be strangers as well to a sense of duty and decorum as to the practice of them. In fine, when children are irregular, vicious, or even sickly, the fault and the misfortune are, in a much higher degree than is usually imagined, attributable to the neglect or mismanagement of those who have had the superintendence of them. You are prepared, I am confident, to concur with me in the sentiment, that some of the greatest difficulties experienced in schools, as relates to every branch of education, arise from the faults of domestic discipline. Let parents and guardians do their duty, and the business of school tuition will not only be facilitated, but enhanced in its usefulness.

Children ought not to be too soon dismissed from an education *exclusively* domestic. They ought not, I mean, to be sent to school at too early an age. A practice the contrary of this threatens to be productive of serious, not to say irreparable mischief. Parents are often too anxious that their children should have a knowledge of the alphabet, of spelling, reading, geography, and other branches of school learning, at a very early age. This is worse than tempting them to walk too early, because the organ likely to be injured by it is much more important than the muscles and bones of the lower extremities. It may do irremediable mischief to the brain. That viscus is yet too immature and feeble to sustain fatigue. Until from the sixth to the eighth year of life, the seventh being perhaps the proper medium, all its energies are necessary for its own healthy development, and that of the other portions of the system. Nor ought they to be diverted, by serious study, to any other purpose. True—exercise is as essential to the health and vigour of the brain, at that time of life, as at any other; but it should be the general and pleasurable exercise of observation and action. It ought not to be the compulsory exercise of tasks. Early prodigies of mind rarely attain mature distinction. The reason is plain: Their brains are injured by premature toil, and their general health impaired. From an unwise attempt to convert at once their flowery spring into a luxuriant summer, that summer too often never arrives. The blossom withers ere the fruit is formed. For these reasons, I have never been an advocate of " Infant Schools." Unless they are conducted with great discretion, they cannot fail to eventuate in mischief. They should be nothing but schools of pleasurable exercise, having little to do with books.

As those institutions are now administered they are serious evils. The passion in favour of them, becoming more extensive in its prevalence, and acquiring daily greater intensity, is among the alarming portents of the time. It is founded on the want of a correct knowledge of the human constitution, and of the amount of labour its different organs can sustain with safety at the different periods of life. Perhaps I should rather say, it is founded on the fallacious belief, that it is the infant's mind *alone* that labours in acquiring school learning, and not any organized portion of his body. This is an error, which, if not corrected, will prove fatal to hundreds of thousands of the human race. It is not the mind but the brain—the master organ of the system, essential to the well-being and efficiency of every other part of it—that toils and is oppressed in the studies of the school. Nor, tender and feeble as it is, is it possible for it to endure the labour often imposed on it, without sustaining irreparable injury—an injury no less subversive of mental than of corporeal soundness and vigour.

Were parents fully sensible of this (a truth which Phrenology alone can teach them), they would no longer overload the brains of their mere babes with study, any more than they would their half-organized muscles and joints with unmerciful burdens of brick and mortar. They would even know that the latter would be the less destructive practice of the two. Under such circumstances we should hear no more of the " Boy's Book," and the " Girl's Book," and the " Child's Own Book," with such other slip-shod, catch-penny trash, as now encumbers our book-stores and parlours. These would all be exchanged for the Book of Nature, which is truly the " Child's Own Book;" and which, being traced for that purpose by the DIVINITY HIMSELF, is faultlessly prepared.

Instead of seeing infants confined to inaction in crowded school-rooms, with saddened looks, moist eyes, and aching heads, we should then meet them in gardens and lawns, groves and pleasure-grounds, breathing wholesome air, leaping, laughing, shouting, cropping flowers, pursuing butterflies, collecting and looking at curious and beautiful insects and stones, listening to bird songs, singing themselves, admiring the bright blue arch of the heavens, or gazing at the thickening folds of the thunder-cloud, and doing all other things fitted to promote health, develope and strengthen their frames, and prepare them for the graver business of after life. And, instead of pale faces, flaccid flesh, and wasted bodies, we should find them with ruddy cheeks, firm muscles, and full and well-rounded limbs.

Exercises and pastimes such as these, constitute the only " Infant School" that deserves to be encouraged; nor will any other sort receive encouragement when the business of education shall be thoroughly understood. The brain of infants will be then no longer neglected as a mass of matter of little importance; skin, muscle, and bone, being thought preferable to it. On the contrary, it will be viewed in its true character, as the ruling organ of the body and the apparatus of the mind, and its training will receive the attention it merits. I repeat—and the repetition should be persevered in until its truth be acknowledged and reduced to practice—that most of the evils of education under which the world has so long suffered, and is still suffering, arise from the mistaken belief, that, in what is called moral and intellectual education, it is the *mind* that is exercised, and not the *brain*. Nor will the evils cease, and education be made perfect, until the error shall be exploded. Knowing nothing of the nature of the mind, and supposing it to be, as a spirit, somewhat *impassive*, we are neither apprized nor apprehensive that any degree of action will impair it. Indeed we can form no conception of an injury done to it as a separate essence. Perhaps the most rational belief is, that it can suffer none. But the case is different as respects organized matter. We witness, daily, injuries done to it by injudicious exercise. Nor is there perhaps any portion of it so easily or ruinously deranged by excessive action as the brain, especially the half-formed and highly susceptible brain of infants. Let this truth be realized, and faithfully and skilfully acted on, and human suffering from hydrocephalus, rickets, phrenitis, idiocy, epilepsy, madness, and other cerebral affections, will be greatly diminished. It would be infinitely wiser and better to employ suitable persons to superintend the exercises and amusements of children under seven years of age, in the fields, orchards, and meadows, and point out to them the riches and beauties of nature, than to have them immured in crowded school-rooms, in a state of inaction, poring over horn-books and primers, conning words of whose meaning they are ignorant, and breathing foul air.*

---

* With respect to the training of infants, we ought to look not only to what is *desirable*, but to what is *practicable*. Were " gardens and lawns, groves and pleasure-grounds," within the reach of the generality of young children residing in large and crowded cities, it might with some shew of reason be said, that in such places most of their time ought to be spent. But the case being otherwise, the best substitute for them must be resorted to; and that substitute, I am convinced, is a rationally conducted infant-school. Nay, such a school I even hold to be far superior to the open fields as a place of habitual resort for children. Dr Caldwell's animadversions are applicable only to those old-fashioned places of confinement, termed " dame's-schools, and " grammar-schools," in which children are kept for many hours together in the same attitude, and poring over books which they do not comprehend. The infant-schools of Owen and Wilderspin are as different from these as day from night. In them the chief attention is devoted to physical education; a large play-ground being provided for this purpose, to which the children are at short intervals dismissed, and where they are found " breathing wholesome air, leaping, laughing, and shouting," as much as Dr Caldwell himself could desire. Even within doors, bodily motion, singing, and shouting, are regularly indulged in. *Lessons* form either a very subordinate part of their employment, or none at all; there is no " poring over horn-books and primers"—no " conning words of whose meaning they are ignorant"—nothing but that exercise of the brain which Dr Caldwell judiciously recommends, " the general and pleasurable exercise of observation and action." The consequence is, that the children, thus trained in accordance with the laws of nature, thrive

After these remarks on what falls more especially within the province of others, I shall now consider briefly a few of those points of physical education in which you, as instructors, have an immediate concern.

and are happy, and, instead of loathing school as under the good old system, look forward with eagerness to the time of returning to it, and cry if detained at home. One great superiority which attendance at such schools possesses over roaming at large in the fields is, that the children are at all times under the eye of the teacher, who trains them to moral habits, fixes moral maxims in their minds, and instantly checks and points out the impropriety of every vicious or selfish act. In this way is " the mind made obedient to discipline and pliant to reason"—the very result which Locke desiderates, and one which could not be brought about if the children were allowed to spend their time in the fields without efficient superintendence. The cultivation of the moral faculties is of very great importance, and can be effected only where there is an assemblage of children, under the guidance of a well-qualified teacher.

It is a safe principle in education, that whatever is productive of misery, and, though rationally taught, requires to be forced upon children, is at variance with the intentions of Nature. Tested in this way, many existing practices are found palpably erroneous. The attention of children ought to be claimed to those subjects only for which the faculties developed at their age are adapted, and the little beings ought not to be tormented with abstract studies which fall within the sphere of powers not unfolded till a later period of life. " This is, however, (to use the words of Dr John Gregory,) so little observed in the education of children of better fashion, that Nature is, almost from the beginning, thwarted in all her motions. Many hours are spent every day in studies painfully disagreeable, that give exercise to no faculty but the memory, and only load it with what will probably never turn to either future pleasure or utility. Some of the faculties are overstrained, by putting them upon exertions disproportioned to their strength; others languish for want of being exercised at all. No knowledge or improvement is here acquired by the free and spontaneous exertion of the natural powers; it is all artificial and forced." Thus health is often sacrificed by the body being deprived of its requisite exercise, the temper hurt by frequent contradiction, and the vigour of the mind impaired by overstraining. The age of cheerfulness and gaiety is spent in the midst of tears, punishments, and slavery, and this to answer no other end but to make a child a man some years before Nature intended he should be one. It is not meant here to insinuate, that children should be left to form themselves without any direction or assistance. On the contrary, we are persuaded they need the most watchful attention from their earliest in-

Having hitherto intentionally omitted it, I find it necessary to my purpose now to observe, that of the sets of organs of which the human body is composed, some are so predominant in their influence, as to assimilate the condition of the others to their own. They exercise, also, a powerful influence over one another. If one of them be deranged, it deranges the others; and if either of them be healthy and vigorous, the soundness of the others may be considered on that account the more secure. Of the control of all and either of them over the rest of the body the same is true. If they be sound, it is sound; if diseased, it is diseased.—To execute the task of physical education, then, it is necessary chiefly so to watch and regulate them, as to keep them unimpaired.

The organs alluded to, as possessing a predominance, are the skin,—the digestive system, composed of the stomach, liver, pancreas, intestines, and lacteals,—the blood-making and blood-circulating system, made up of the heart, lungs, and blood-vessels,—and the cerebral and nervous system, comprising the brain, spinal cord, and nerves. The muscular system is also important, not only in itself, but as contributing, by its functions, to the perfection of the others. Physical education, as an aggregate, then, consists in the proper education of these several sets of organs. Train them in the best manner, and to the highest pitch, and the individual has attained his highest perfection.

fancy, and that they often contract such bad health, such bad tempers, and such bad habits, before they are thought proper subjects of education, as will remain with them, in spite of all future care, as long as they live. We only intended to point out the impropriety of precipitating education, in forsaking the order in which nature unfolds the human powers, and of sacrificing present happiness to uncertain futurity. There is a kind of culture that will produce a man at fifteen with his character and manners perfectly formed: but he is a little man; his faculties are cramped, and he is incapable of further improvement. By a different culture he might not perhaps arrive at his full maturity till five-and-twenty; but then he would be by far the superior man—bold, active, and vigorous, with all his powers capable of farther enlargement." (*Comparative View, &c.* p. 58—60).—R. C.

Of the *education of the skin* I have already spoken, under the heads of cleanliness, clothing, and temperature; for the chief action of temperature is on that organ. On these points, therefore, I have but little to add. The same attention to them required in the nursery, is required in the school. The temperature of school-rooms should be comfortable in all sorts of weather, and the cleanliness and clothing of pupils such as may best contribute to the health of the skin. The rooms themselves should also be clean. The covering of all children, especially of delicate ones, had better be too warm than too cool. And pupils should never be allowed to sit in school with their clothes and feet wet, or even damp. The most vigorous constitutions have suffered from such exposure. Persons may *exercise* with impunity, in damp clothing, and with wet feet, but not *sit still*. Nor should children be exposed to currents of air in school-rooms. They would be safer out of doors than under the action of such a cause.

The *education of the digestive organs* has been briefly noticed under the head of diet. It is matter of regret to me, that time does not permit me to enlarge on it, as it is infinitely important in physical education. Long-lived individuals are generally remarkable for the soundness of their stomachs. Many of them have never experienced nausea, and rarely an impaired appetite. Improprieties in diet are the most fruitful source of the diseases of children. Nor are they much less so to those of riper age. Eating too much, and of unwholesome articles, is a national evil in the United States; and were I to add, a national disgrace, the charge would scarcely be too severe. Do you ask me whether it is more so in the United States than elsewhere? I answer, Yes; and the reason is manifest. Such is our happy condition, did we not abuse it, that it is much easier to procure the means of indulging to excess in the United States than in any other country. And experience, in common with history, teaches us, that mankind are prone to the gratification of the palate, and other animal appetites, in proportion to the facilities of indulgence they enjoy. I confidently believe, that the thirteen or fourteen millions of people inhabiting this country, eat more trash, *for amusement*, and *fashion's sake*, and to *pass away idle time*, than half the inhabitants of Europe united. Unquestionably they consume a greater amount of such articles, in the proportion of *five to one*, than an equal number of the people of any other country I have ever visited. Shame, if not prudence, should drive them from a practice which might well be called disgusting. No wonder that European travellers ridicule us on account of it. In a special manner should children and youth be guarded from its influence, calculated as it is to weaken their constitutions and injure their intellects, and thus reduce the man of America below the standard he would otherwise attain. Nor will human nature ever reach the perfection our fine climate, abundance of wholesome food, entire freedom of mind and body, and other favourable influences belonging to our country, would bestow on it, unless the evil be remedied. For, that the Americans have it in their power, if they be true to themselves and use with wisdom the advantages they enjoy, to become, bodily and mentally, the most perfect people the world has produced, might be easily shewn, had I leisure to sum up the evidence which presents itself.

It is well known to every teacher, that children are comparatively dull after dinner, and often sleep over their tasks. Why? Because they have dined on improper food, or eaten to excess of that which is proper. In such a case, the exercise of the brain, or of the mind, if the latter word be preferred, proves injurious, by producing indigestion. It expends, in the organ of thought, that portion of vitality which should now centre in the stomach, to enable it to master the enemy within it—to convert the oppressive load of food it has received into chyme, and prepare it for chyle. Daily assaults of this sort on the brain (especially the tender brain of children, which is not completely organized), by errors in diet, cannot fail to do it permanent mischief. But, as already observed, the regulation of the diet of children belongs chiefly to family government. As respects the serious evils, however, arising from errors committed in it, teachers should be neither inattentive nor silent. Due representations and remonstrances, made by them to parents and guardians, might be productive of good. They have a better opportunity than most other persons, to witness the unfavourable effect which the practice objected to produces on the mind.

Those organs of the body to which the attention of teachers should be more immediately and earnestly directed, are the lungs, the heart and blood-vessels, the muscles of voluntary motion, and the brain and nerves.

The chief measure requisite in the *education of the lungs*, is the procurement for pupils of a competent supply of salubrious atmospherical air. And I need scarcely add, that to remain salubrious it must be regularly changed. Independently of any deleterious impregnation it may receive, stagnation alone injures air as certainly as water. The object here referred to involves the most important considerations, as it is impossible for health to be secured without it. The attainment of it depends principally on the site and construction of school-edifices. The buildings should stand in elevated, dry, and healthy positions, remote from swamps, and low, humid, alluvial soil. Or, if there be such nuisances in the vicinity, rows of bushy trees should run between them and the houses; the latter being erected on the windward side—on that side, I mean, over which the prevailing winds of summer and autumn pass, before they reach the miasmatic ground. On no account, if it can be avoided, should a schoolhouse stand in a flat, damp, alluvial situation. And should there be no preventive of this, let the edifice be erected on an artificial hillock, or in some other way elevated fifteen or twenty feet above the level of the ground. By this means, the pupils, being placed beyond the reach of the miasm that may be formed below them, will breathe a wholesome atmosphere. A stagnant atmosphere, however, as already mentioned, cannot long remain wholesome, more especially if it be charged with animal exhalations. To prevent, therefore, in schools, these two sources of mischief, the rooms should never be crowded, and ought to be so constructed that their ventilation may be perfect without rendering their temperature uncomfortable in cold weather. This state of things, so highly desirable and so easily attained, is not usually found in houses of instruction for junior pupils. On the contrary, the rooms are for the most part crowded, sometimes jammed with children; too hot in winter when the windows are closed, and too cold, and swept by currents of chilling air, when they are open. In such places, delicate children, especially if their lungs be more than commonly sensitive, can scarcely fail to contract disease. Or, should they escape actual disease, their delicacy and feebleness will be increased. For the preservation of health and vigour when possessed, and their restoration when lost, a supply of salubrious air is as necessary to the lungs as a supply of sound and nutritious aliment is to the stomach. The one is not more essential to the production of healthy chyle, than the other is to the formation of healthy blood. And we shall endeavour to shew presently, that, without such blood, not a single function belonging to man, whether it be physical, intellectual, or moral, can be in unimpaired health and perfection; for, heterodox as the sentiment may probably appear to some persons, it is, notwithstanding, true, that florid, well vitalized arterial blood, is as necessary to give full vigour to the intellectual and moral powers of the philosopher, statesman, and patriot, as it is to paint the roses on the virgin's cheek, and the coral on her lip. The reason is plain. That they may be in the best condition to perform their functions, the intellectual and moral organs, like other portions of the body, require a supply of well-prepared blood; and to form such blood is the province of the lungs, using, as their principal means, unadulterated atmospherical air. Other things being alike, the more perfect the blood, the brighter is perception, and the more vigorous every mental operation. These assertions are susceptible of proof. Shall I be told, in opposition to this sentiment, that men of the most brilliant and powerful minds have often very feeble and shattered health, and that therefore their brains are not supplied with well-prepared blood? I reply that the objection has no weight. The intellects of the individuals referred to are always in the best condition, and work most powerfully when corporeal health and vigour are least impaired. In other words, the more perfect the blood that goes to the brain, and the better that organ is sustained by the sound sympathies of other parts, the more healthfully and vigorously does it perform its functions. Though, on account of their cerebral organization, such men are great without very good blood, they would be greater with it.

You have already been informed, that to the formation of good blood a due supply of pure atmospherical air is indispensably requisite. But no room, even moderately filled with human beings, can retain a pure atmosphere, however judiciously it may be constructed for ventilation. Children, therefore, should be confined in such a place but a few hours at a time, and not many hours in the entire day. That they may enjoy perfect health, a considerable portion of their time should be passed in the open air. There the food of their lungs will be wholesome and their respiration free, and they will derive from that function all the benefit it is calculated to bestow.

Another useful measure, in the education of the lungs, is for pupils to practise declamation and singing. Such training strengthens those organs as certainly as suitable exercise strengthens the muscles, and it does it on the same ground. I again repeat, and it can hardly be too often repeated, that it is well-directed exercise alone that invigorates and improves every form of living matter. Its effect thus to invigorate and improve, constitutes one of its most important laws. Nor is its ameliorating influence confined to living matter. It improves dead matter also. By judicious use, a bow grows better; and to the improvement of violins, flutes, organs, pianos, and other musical instruments, by being skilfully played on, all experience testifies.

As respects the salutary influence of singing, declamation, and other forms of loud speaking, on the lungs, Dr Rush often said, and perhaps has left the fact on record, that, in the experience of a long life, he had never known a singing-schoolmaster, an auction-crier, a watchman who called the hours of the night, or an oysterman who cried his commodity through the streets, to be attacked by pulmonary consumption. The influence of declamation by the sea-shore, amidst the roar of the surf, in strengthening the lungs of Demosthenes, might be cited as testifying to the same effect.

The mere formation of good blood, however, is not alone sufficient to satisfy all the demands of the system. That fluid must be also circulated actively to every portion of the body, else the purposes of vigorous health are not subserved by it. To this end the free and competent action of the heart is essential; and to that again, voluntary muscular action is no less so. However useful well-vitalized arterial blood is as a stimulant to excite the left side of the heart to the requisite degree of motion, experience proves that it is not alone sufficient for the purpose. Every one knows, that when he is motionless, his pulse is slow and comparatively feeble, contrasted with itself when he is engaged in exercise. So is his respiration. Even when our exercise is moderate, we inspire a third or fourth oftener, in a given time, than we do when we are still. Our inspirations are also deeper and fuller. More air, therefore, is received in an equal period into the lungs. But, other things being alike, the larger the volume of air that enters those organs, the more completely is the blood vitalized and matured; and, if correspondingly circulated, the more efficiently does it contribute to the perfection of every function of the system. Hence the health, vivacity, strength, and florid complexions of persons, whether children or adults, who exercise and respire freely in the open air; and the comparative paleness, delicate health, languor, and weakness of those who pass their time in a state of inaction, even in the most spacious and comfortable dwellings. This truth is amply illustrated and confirmed, by contrasting the agriculturist, who labours in the field, or the hunter, who roams the forest, with the secluded man of letters, or with the manufacturer who closely pursues his occupation in a small and ill-ventilated workshop.

In all parts of the world, and under all circumstances, highly studious and literary men have infirm health. The reason is plain. They exercise their brains too much, and their muscles, hearts, and lungs too little. Hence the whole frame is first debilitated, and ultimately deranged. The lungs and heart failing somewhat in their functions, the brain does not receive a sufficient amount of well-vitalized blood. Its vigour is diminished, therefore, by a two-fold cause ; exhaustion from its excessive labours, and a defective supply of sound arterial blood, which is its *vital food*. Though, in a given time, then, a literary man may accomplish a greater amount of work by inordinate and unremitting cerebral toil, he cannot do it so well. In a particular manner, the product of his mind will have less brilliancy and power. It will be like the fruit of advanced age, contrasted with that of the meridian of life—like the Odyssey of Homer, compared to the Iliad, or Milton's Paradise Regained, to his Paradise Lost. Another cause of the infirm health of literary men is, that they eat too much, or indulge in food too difficult of digestion. This renders them dyspeptic. Their stomachs being debilitated in common with their other organs, the diet used by them should be of the most digestible kind ; and it should be taken sparingly. Let such characters take more muscular exercise in the open air, and eat less, and they will enjoy much more health of body and vigour and productiveness of mind.*

* The advice here given by Dr Caldwell is of peculiar importance to theologians, whose professional duties require not merely efficient intellectual faculties, but great vigour of the lungs and muscular system. No course of training for the clerical profession ought to overlook

As heretofore mentioned, light itself, which acts on us more freely, and to better effect, without doors than within, is friendly to both vegetable and animal perfection.

these important organs; and no one accustomed to ground his judgments on philosophical principles, instead of slavish custom, will regard the affirmation as extravagant, that the practice of some art requiring much exercise of the lungs and thoracic muscles, ought everywhere to form a branch of clerical education. Were this suggestion followed, the public would witness more rarely than they do the melancholy spectacle of a young man of talent utterly ruining his health, and destroying his usefulness, within a few years after beginning to preach, by exacting from his lungs and muscles an amount of labour which, though necessary, they are altogether unable to perform. That there is nothing chimerical in this view, is satisfactorily demonstrated by actual experiment made in the United States of America. On 1st May 1829 there was opened at Germantown, near Philadelphia, an institution called the Manual Labour Academy of Pennsylvania. Its principal design is to furnish pious and indigent youths, at little or no expense, with the means of education for the ministry, and at the same time to invigorate their bodies, and give them industrious and moral habits. The leading feature is the *union of academic studies with systematic bodily labour;* each pupil being required to work three or four hours every day at farming, gardening, or some mechanical occupation. The following extracts from the first Report of the institution, published at Philadelphia in 1829, will be read with interest:—

" The premises consist of forty-two and a half acres of good land, several outhouses, and a commodious dwelling on the main street, the residence of the late Dr Blair. The farm is in the rear of the dwelling, opening on a lane which communicates with the main road; there is on it stabling, a coach-house, granary, cart-shed, and farm-yard, and a culinary garden of one-third of an acre.

" The youth have respectable talents, habitual industry, and are well pleased with the mode of education. The health of this interesting family has been uninterrupted, except in a few cases, diseased when admitted. Every invalid remaining there has been restored to health. They board with the Principal; their diet is plain, and in as great variety as is consistent with economy and health, and as much as possible the product of the pupils' labours on the farm. Piety, learning, and honest industry, are here united. Surely such an enterprise cannot fail.

" The usual branches of study in classical schools are pursued, with the addition of the study of the Bible. The hours of recreation are not hours of waste, and idleness, and immorality. They are employed

Shut up in *entire* darkness either man, quadrupeds, or birds, and you injure and enfeeble them. Casper Hauser, Baron Trenck, and many other persons that might

in useful bodily labour; such as will exercise their skill, make them dexterous, establish their health and strength, enable each one to defray his own expenses, and fit him for the vicissitudes of life; particularly so, if they be destined for our new settlements as Christian missionaries.

" Thus far they have been employed in carpenter-work, gardening, and farming. Four of the *students* are *good workmen in wood;* profitable in their own labour, and also as instructors to those who are less experienced. Six or seven thus employed have already made the various repairs of the building, and nearly *all the needful furniture.* Some orders from the city for small wooden articles have been executed by them, and they are ready for more. Those who are engaged in gardening have supplied the house. Others will furnish from the farm thirty bushels of wheat, seventy bushels of rye, ten tons of hay, one hundred and fifty bushels of corn, and three hundred and fifty bushels of potatoes."

At the time of the publication of the Report, the number of scholars was twenty-five. The institution was superintended by two gentlemen (a principal and professor of mathematics), who resided in it with their families, and took charge of the pupils as of one great domestic circle. The results of the manual labour upon the young men are thus described :—" Their blood flows warm, and rich, and equable; and the east winds cannot penetrate them. Their thirst demands water, their hunger plain food; their limbs rejoice in muscular efforts, and their minds in truth. Sleep rests them, and their waking eyes behold the light of another cheerful useful day. These are some of the blessings. And ought not the land of Christian pilgrims to have many such institutions?"

The Report goes on to mention some very striking and important facts, which are so much to our present purpose that no apology is necessary for quoting them at full length :—

" For twenty years and more the unnatural union of sedentary with studious habits, contracted by the monastic system, has been killing in the middle age. The Register of Education shews, in one year, one hundred and twenty-one deaths. Examine into the particular cases, and these will be found the undoubted effects of sedentary habits. Look at one name there. He had valuable gifts, perfected by two years' academic, four years' collegiate, and three years' theological studies. He preached, gave much promise, and then died of a stomach disease. He contracted it when a student. He did not alternate bodily with mental labour, or he had lived and been a bless-

be named, furnish memorable examples of this. *Partial* darkness, therefore, must produce on them an effect differing only in degree. It has been observed, that, other

ing to the church. When he entered on his studies, he was growing into full size and strength. He sat down till his muscles dwindled, his digestion became disordered, his chest contracted, his lungs congested, and his head liable to periodical pains. He sat four years in college, and three years in theological application. *Look at him now.* He has gained much useful knowledge, and has improved his talents; but he has lost his health. The duties of his mind and heart were done, and faithfully so; but those of his body were left undone. Three hundred and seventy muscles, organs of motion, have been robbed of their appropriate action for nine or ten years, and now they have become, alike with the rest of his frame, the prey of near one hundred and fifty diseased and irritable nerves. And he soon dies of a disease, as common and fashionable of late as the studio-sedentary habit—a disease caused by muscular inaction. Look at another case. Exposure, incident to the parson or missionary, has developed the disease in his chest, planted there when fitting himself for usefulness. He contracted a sedentary, while he was gaining a studious habit. That which he sows that shall he also reap. The east winds give him colds; a pulpit effort causes hoarseness and cough, oppression and pain. He becomes alarmed and nervous. His views of usefulness begin to be limited. He must now go by direction, and not so much to labour, where otherwise he would have been most wanted, as to nurse his broken constitution; and he soon adds to the lamentable list of *mysterious providences*—to the number of innocent victims, rather, of cultivating the mind and heart at the unnecessary and sinful expense of the body— to the number of loud calls to alternate mental and corporeal action daily, for the reciprocal sanity and vigour of both mind and body.

" Why is the manual-labour system so abandoned? The child alternates his period of morning and afternoon confinement by his various cheerful amusements in the open air. But, when the animal frame is developed, and the redundancy of life and spirits is expended, how, let it be asked with solicitude, is the tendency to muscular action, which yet remains, satisfied, when the childlike exercises are put aside? In what manner is exhausted the health-preserving impulse to bodily activity? With what do students generally alternate their periods of study? Some allow themselves no relaxation, except what eating, and sleep, and recitation, and casual conversation, may afford. Too many alternate study with sensuality; while others, more methodical, take set walks, make reluctant and fruitless resolutions to split and saw fuelwood, and, less willingly, when the novelty is over, to beat and move their muscles around a gymnasium. These efforts at muscular exercise,

things being equal, dark work-shops are less salubrious than well-lighted ones. To the perfection of our race, then, liberal exercise in the open air—a much larger

too artificial to be lasting and suitable, declare, too plainly to be misunderstood, that a defect exists in our present collegiate system—a defect remediable only by natural and useful employment.

" This health-preserving labour is also *profitable*, and its results are placed by the Board of Trustees to the credit of each *manual-labour student*. By the Board's estimate, made in August last (when the institution had been opened scarcely four months), several pupils were found to have very small balances against them for their boarding and tuition, and some of them had almost none; notwithstanding the charges are, owing to the location of the school, higher than in the interior parts of our country.

" The Manual Labour Academy of Pennsylvania is not a solitary institution. Similar ones are in Prussia, Germany, and Switzerland; in five places in our own country, and more are in contemplation. It is not an *ephemeral novelty*, but a lasting improvement in the system of modern education. At Whitesborough, N. Y., there is one of between thirty and forty pupils. At Andover, Mass., another which already accommodates near sixty pupils. At Princeton, Kentucky, there is a third, which now contains eighty pupils. A fourth exists at Maysville, Tenessee. It is reported that the Methodist brethren intend one in Maine. The Bloomfield seminary of New Jersey is expected soon to be modelled on this plan; and permanent efforts are now making to establish an extensive manual labour school at Cincinnati, Ohio. At the lowest estimate, there are now (1829), in the process of education, two hundred and one youth of our country on the manual labour plan."

One great advantage attending these seminaries is, that the pupils work in each other's society. This mode of exercise is far more beneficial than solitary labour, conversation being extremely useful in refreshing and invigorating the minds of the pupils, and turning their thoughts into new channels. Society, moreover, gives a pleasing excitement to various of the cerebral organs, which is eminently favourable to health and mental vivacity. It is mentioned in the Report, that those pupils who are fondest of their manual employments, and improve most rapidly in dexterity and skill, make at the same time most improvement in their studies. On the whole, the system pursued at the Manual Labour Academies appears to be so much in accordance with sound physiology, and so clearly beneficial in its results, that little doubt can be entertained of its being speedily introduced into Britain; and it is in the hope that the present note may be instrumental in hastening the occurrence of so desirable an event that the subject is here protractedly dwelt upon.—R. C.

amount of it than is taken by children at school, especially female children—is essential. Never will mankind attain the high standard, either bodily or mental, of which they are susceptible, until females, not only while children, but also during adult life, take more and freer exercise out of doors than they do at present. I do not mean that they ought to run foot-races, wrestle, spar, fence, vault over six-bar gates, or in any other way hoiden it. Such masculine feats would suit neither their taste, delicacy, nor intended pursuits; nor are they requisite. No: I mean that they should, as a duty to themselves, their contemporaries, and posterity, indulge in graceful and becoming exercise, in the streets, gardens, fields, lawns, roads, and pleasure-grounds, to a sufficient extent to invigorate their frames, heighten their beauty, and strengthen their intellects. Should they even climb lofty hills and craggy mountains, breathe the pure air, and enjoy the spirit-stirring and inspiring prospects they afford, the excursions would be beneficial both to body and mind. For, I repeat, exercise, judiciously directed and indulged in, improves the latter as certainly as the former. Walking, then, is one excellent form of exercise for females, and riding on horse-back is another. It is praiseworthy in them, moreover, to learn to walk elegantly, because graceful motion adds to their accomplishments, and increases their attractiveness. The air of Josephine, in walking, was fascination; and an American lady, now in London, threw a spell over royalty by the grace of her movement in quitting the drawing-room. But by *elegance* in walking, I do not mean primness, mincingness, or any thing artificial. Far from it. Let all be natural; but nature should be cultivated and improved. Let ladies afford reason to have said of them, what the poet of Abbotsford says of his Ellen Douglas:

> "A foot more light, a step more true,
> Ne'er from the heath-flower brushed the dew;
> E'en the slight hare-bell reared its head,
> Elastic from her airy tread."

In truth, that same lovely Ellen, though reared on a secluded island amidst the Highlands of Scotland, was mistress of many other attributes, several of them the mere result of health, and that health the product of lake and mountain exercise, which the most high-bred and courtly female might be excused for envying. For the same poet, who, had he written nothing else, has immortalized himself by immortalizing her, farther tells us, that—

> " Ne'er did Grecian chisel trace
> A nymph, a naiad, or a grace,
> With finer form, or lovelier face.
> What though the sun, with ardent frown,
> Had slightly tinged her cheek with brown,
> The sportive toil which, short and light,
> Had dyed her glowing hue so bright,
> Served, too, in hastier swell to shew
> Short glimpses of a breast of snow.
> And seldom o'er a breast so fair
> Mantled a plaid with modest care;
> And never brooch the folds combined
> Above a heart more good and kind.
> Her kindness and her worth to spy,
> You need but look in Ellen's eye:
> Not Katrine, in her mirror blue,
> Gives back the shaggy banks more true,
> Than every freeborn glance confessed
> The guileless movements of her breast;
> Whether joy sparkled in her eye,
> Or woe or pity claimed a sigh,
> Or filial love was glowing there,
> Or meek devotion poured a prayer,
> Or tale of injury called forth
> The indignant spirit of the north.—
> One only passion unrevealed,
> With maiden pride the maid concealed,
> Yet not less purely felt the flame—
> Oh! need I tell that passion's name!"

Carriage-riding is, at best, a semi-sedentary occupation, and does but little good in imparting strength. A lady possessed of a fine figure, who dresses with taste and rides gracefully, never appears to more advantage than when seated on an elegant and well-gaited horse. Nor can she indulge in a more salutary mode of exercise. For younger females, it is equally beneficial. As riding on horseback, moreover, requires some boldness of spirit, the practice tends to lessen that female timidity which is often inconvenient and injurious to its possessors, as well as to others. However desirable sensibility may be in a reasonable degree, like all other qualities it may become excessive, turn to evil, and impair health. Experience teaches us that it often does so, especially in feeble persons, in whom it is most prone to become inordinate, *on account* of their feebleness. To restrain it, therefore, so as to hold it within due bounds, by invigorating exercise, and judicious exposure to something bordering on danger, or at least resembling it, is an end that should be constantly aimed at in the physical education of females, and also of males who have any thing of feminine susceptibility in their temperaments. Peter the Great had an instinctive dread of water, of which he was cured by being repeatedly precipitated into rivers. On the same principles, Frederick III. had a troublesome excess of sensitiveness obliterated.

That it may be useful in the highest degree, exercise ought not to be very severe. It should not amount to labour or straining. A form of it so violent, if it does no actual organic mischief, diminishes vitality by an excessive expenditure of it, instead of augmenting it. Like excess in every thing else, it is wrong and injurious, *because* of its excess; hence some of the violent gymnastic exploits practised occasionally in seats of learning, are better calculated to do harm than good. Though they produce salutary action in some of the muscles, they strain, exhaust, and injure others. Those who take exercise for the sake of health and vigour, especially if they be delicate, should never carry it so far, either in violence or duration, as to induce fatigue. In a higher or lower degree, that is dangerous, and may prove the cause of actual sickness. The manual-labour system connected with some schools, is not only more useful in its objects, but better fitted to subserve health than the common gymnastic one. Still the moderate and graceful gymnastic exercises are so useful and desirable, as the source of accomplishments, that I should regret their abolishment. One of the best forms of them is that of the sword, especially the small-sword. It is at once elegant, invigorating, and manly, giving fine play to all the principal muscles of the body.

Nor does it, as some imagine, foster a propensity to combat and blood. Far from it. That feeling belongs only to the bully and the ruffian. While a knowledge of the art of defence increases personal firmness and self-reliance in cases of difficulty and danger, it is usually accompanied by a pacific temper and a gentlemanly disposition. Nor can it well be otherwise. A fencing-school, properly conducted, is a place of polished courtesy, and therefore an institution peculiarly fitted for the cultivation of a graceful deportment, suavity of manners, and amenity of disposition. Football and handball are useful exercises; so is swimming, when it can be properly practised. Besides giving vigour to the muscles, the latter contributes to health by promoting cleanliness. It need scarcely be added, that the action of salt water on the skin, when it can be had, is considered preferable to that of fresh. It is a current and probably a well-founded belief, that habitual sea-bathing co-operates with the purity of a marine atmosphere in bestowing on islanders their unbroken healthfulness and great longevity.

As an in-door exercise, for both males and females, nothing is superior to dancing. Besides the grace of movement which it teaches, it gives action and excitement to the whole frame, the music and social intercourse contributing their part to the general effect. If it sometimes does mischief by being carried to excess, that is an abuse of it, and does not justly bring reproach on its proper use, or furnish evidence that it ought to be discarded. As well might the use of food be discarded, because many persons abuse it by eating too much. Ten thousand people injure themselves by the abuse of eating, for one who does so by that of dancing.* The exercise of

* Dancing is of great service in dispelling low spirits. Persons sub-

swinging by the arms, if judiciously practised, is beneficial, especially to those who have weak chests. So is that of the dumb-bells, with various others to which time does not allow me to refer.

It is of moment to observe, that severe exercise should never be taken during hot weather, or immediately after a plentiful meal. In the former case, the excitement of the exercise, added to that of the heat, has double force in exhausting vitality and weakening the body; and, in the latter, too much cerebral influence, for the time, being expended in muscular action, the amount of it conveyed to the stomach is insufficient for the laborious function that viscus has to perform; and indigestion is the consequence. This fact constitutes the foundation of the Spaniard's *siesta*, and of the repose which, under the guidance of instinct, most of the inferior animals take after a copious repast. On the same ground, the savage of our forests, after over-gorging himself, often consumes a natural day in the sleep of digestion. But it is a dreamy sleep, the brain being disturbed by the toils of the stomach. It is the source of those visions of war and hunting, which, occurring in the brave, are often received as premonitions to action.

Such are some of the useful effects of muscular exercise, but not the whole of them. To speak summarily of it. By its aid, in maturing, vitalizing, and circulating the blood, that form of exercise contributes to the vitality of the whole system, to the size and tone of every organ, and the soundness and vigour of every function of it, the moral and intellectual ones not excepted. Nor is this all. Added to its enlarging and strengthening the muscles themselves, it gives them a promptitude and an adroitness of action, important in most of the concerns of life. What is man without a vigorous and well-trained system of muscles?—instruments which he can turn,

ject to mental depression, especially if they enjoy few opportunities of mixing with agreeable society, will find it extremely beneficial, when the labours of the day are over, to join an evening class of adult pupils in a dancing-school.—R. C.

with ease and effect, to any occupation in which his fortune may summon him to engage?—which he can apply, at will, to matters of business, pastime, or pleasure? Without such muscular discipline and power, he would be wretched in himself, and a cipher in the world. Nor is the whole yet told. Elegance and symmetry of person, beauty of complexion, vivacity and force of expression, grace of motion, and all else that is attractive in human nature, depend, in a high degree, on well-directed muscular exercise.

Much is said about matter being a clog on mind; and that the soul is incarcerated within the body, like a prisoner in his cell. The sentiment is as impious as it is untrue. Matter clog and incarcerate mind, and prevent it from acting in a manner suitable to its powers! The assertion is a slander on HIM who made and governs both mind and matter. If the inferior substance be thus prejudicial to the superior, and so unworthy of it as many pronounce it, why did the Deity link them together? No good motive could have led Him to this; and who will dare to charge Him with an evil one? Did He unite them through inadvertence or mistake, or because He did not know what influence matter would have on mind until He had made the experiment; or, did they, when created, rush together forcibly, He having no power to restrain them? Did He yoke them in sport and wantonness, that they might fall to civil war, and try which could do the other most harm, He enjoying their strife and suffering as an amusement? Or, was His motive a desire to show how unharmoniously and incongruously He could pack the works of creation together? No one will *openly* impute to Him faults or weaknesses like these. Yet all *virtually* do that, or something worse, who pronounce matter a hinderance to mind, in any of its operations. For aught that man can show to the contrary, mind would be as imbecile without matter, as matter would be without mind. What can the latter do without the aid of the former? Can it see, hear, taste, smell, feel, or move? Can it lift a pound weight, make a pin or a pen, or use them if already made—think, reason, judge, or perform a single useful act, intellectual or moral, theoretical or practical? If it can, let that act be specified and proved. I say " proved;" because I wish for *realities*, not *suppositions* or *fancies*. I know we are told that the mind can do wonders without the body—that it can traverse all space with more than lightning's speed—outstrip light, in journeying from world to world, to study and enjoy the beauties, sublimities, and grandeur of the universe;—that, were it disencumbered of the shackles of matter, all creation would be subject to its inspection, ministering immediately to its information and delight:— all these things, and many more, are *told* to us. But they are *only* told. They are not *proved*. Far from it. The *contrary* is proved, by evidence which we cannot doubt. All that the mind has any knowledge of, is matter; of spirit, as already stated, it knows nothing. And all the means it employs to acquire knowledge, are matter. It sees with a material eye, hears with a material ear, thinks with a material brain, and moves from place to place, in quest of information and pleasure, with material muscles and bones. Every implement, moreover, in addition to those received from nature, which it uses either in science or art, is of matter. The mechanician works *with* matter, *on* matter. The chemist analyzes matter by matter. The navigator triumphs by matter over the world of waters, which are themselves matter; and the astronomer scans the heavens with nothing else. Nor does saying and believing all this amount to materialism. Or if it does, materialism is truth; and, regardless of names, that is all I want. The entire doctrine comes to this, and nothing more:—mind, being the superior agent, uses matter to effect purposes it could not attain without it; as the chieftain gains a victory with his soldiers, which he could not achieve alone. He is as really the governing spirit of his army, as the mind is of the human body. It will be understood and remembered, that I have been speaking of mind in our present state of being. The discussion of its powers and prerogatives in a future state is the province of others.

The inference to be deduced from the premises just stated is, that physical education, which consists in the cultivation and improvement of our material organs, is a work infinitely more important than it is generally supposed to be. In fact, it alone, according as it is well or ill conducted, can raise human nature to the highest pitch of perfection of which it is susceptible, or sink it to the lowest point of degradation. No language, therefore, can too strongly recommend, nor any measures too strictly enforce, the duty of practising it.

The *physical education of the brain* shall now be the subject of a few remarks. I say " physical," for it is as susceptible of that form of education as any other organ. So true is this, that it is the *only form it can receive.* And were that brought to perfection, nothing more could be done, nor would aught more be requisite, for the improvement of mind. For, as already mentioned and explained, cerebral and mental education are the same.*
Here, again, I must speak as a phrenologist; for in no other capacity can I treat rationally of the subject I am about to consider.

Like all other parts of the system, the brain, by suitable and well-regulated exercise, is enlarged, invigorated, rendered more dexterous in action, and therefore improved in every respect as the organ of the mind. This is as certain as it is that the muscles themselves are improved by training. And, as is the case with other organs, it also may be exhausted and injured by too much and enfeebled by too little action. For it should never be forgotten or neglected, as a practical truth, that, as action strengthens and improves living matter, inaction deteriorates and weakens it. That is one of the leading principles by which physical education is to be directed. Indeed it constitutes its foundation.

* To the *education* or *training* of the organs of the intellectual faculties, however, must be added *instruction*, or the communication of knowledge which the intellect stores up.—R. C.

The brain is not a simple but a compound organ. I should rather say, that it is an aggregate of many smaller organs, distinct from each other, yet closely linked in their condition by sympathy. The soundness of one of them aids in giving soundness to the others, and the converse. These organs, being the instruments of separate mental faculties, are destined to the performance of separate functions, no one of them being able to perform any other function than its own; as the eye sees but cannot hear, and the ear hears but can neither taste nor smell. As these organs, which unite in making up the cerebral mass, execute different sorts of work, so can they work at different times, some of them being active while others are at rest. In this, again, they resemble the external senses: for the ear may be impressed with sound, while the eyes are closed; the eye may see, while the ears are closed; and the sense of smell may be active, while that of touch is dormant. The cerebral organs, moveover, like the external senses, are excited to action by different objects and kinds of impression. Thus, the eye is acted on only by light, the ear by sound, and the smell, taste, and touch, by odorous, sapid, and tangible matter. In like manner, one cerebral organ is acted on and exercised by language; another by form or figure; a third by size; a fourth by number; a fifth by place; a sixth by tune; a seventh and eighth by objects and events; a ninth by colour; and others again by the agents appropriate to them. Each one, however, can be acted on and exercised only by things in its own line—by such, I mean, as specially correspond to it. The same organ, for example, which takes cognizance of size, and is exercised by it, cannot be excited by form; nor can that which is acted on by number be influenced by tune, time, or place. And thus of all the others.

The organs I have here named, are intellectual ones. There are organs again of animal propensity, such as love,* resentment, covetousness, cunning; and others of

* The reader will understand that the cerebral organs here referred to are named in common language, best suited to those to whom the

moral sentiment, as benevolence, veneration, justice, and firmness.* These may likewise be excited to action, strengthened, and improved, each by its own peculiar agent and form of impression; and they may all be enfeebled by a state of inaction. For I again repeat, that it is suitable action alone which amends living matter, including that of every description, while a want of action deteriorates it to the same extent.

The human brain thus consisting, as I have just stated, of three compartments, the animal, the moral, and the intellectual—to raise the mental character to the highest perfection, each of these must be large, well-organized, and healthy, and a correct balance must subsist between them. To a solid and infallible foundation for strength and activity of intellect, sound morality, and energy of character, nothing else is necessary. Skilful training, by turning to the proper account these high gifts of nature, and in that way engrafting improvement on capacity, will finish the work. Were the whole human race thus happily tempered, the condition of man would be as perfect as it could be rendered, and the state of society correspondingly prosperous. Talent and knowledge would prevail and be respected, morality and active virtue would predominate over profligacy and vice, and that every one should be happy in himself and useful to others, would be the ambition and earnest endeavour of all. This would be a millennium,

---

discourse was addressed. Technically, they are Amativeness, Combativeness, Acquisitiveness, Secretiveness, Benevolence, Veneration, Conscientiousness, and Firmness. [Resentment appears to arise rather from Destructiveness than from Combativeness. See *Phrenological Journal*, vol. ix. p. 501.—R. C.]

* It is very questionable whether Firmness is entitled to the appellation of a moral sentiment. There is nothing inherently moral in a mere *tendency to persist*; since it may lead either to good or to evil consequences, according as it is well or ill directed by other faculties. Only those powers which discriminate between right and wrong, ought to be denominated moral sentiments—namely, Benevolence, Veneration, and Conscientiousness.—R. C.

brought into existence by means of education, and in conformity to the constitution of human nature. And let that state of improved being occur when it may, the perfect organization of man, more especially of his brain, will constitute its basis. Let me not be misunderstood in this assertion; in a special manner, let it not be imagined that I intend by it any irreverence toward the Christian religion. Far from it. My meaning is, that whatever agency, divine or human, may bring about in man the change productive of a millennial condition, that change will consist in an improved organization—an organization *made perfect*—by influence FROM ABOVE, if it be so ordained, and if that be the only source from which such influence can proceed—or by means of education, perfect in its principles, and suitably administered. To me the latter appears most probable; because it is most in accordance with the grounds of other changes and improvements in the great dispensation under which we live. It is the amendment of man's earthly condition by his own exertions; and there is no reason to believe that it is amended at present, or intended to be hereafter, in any other way. Nor ought it to be. If, possessing, as he does, the capacity and the means, man will not labour for the improvement of his nature, he is unworthy of it; nor, as I confidently believe, will he ever receive it as a gratuity. But, come the amending power from what quarter it may, men, to be fit members of the millennium, must have the fine organization of John, the beloved disciple, rather than that of Judas, which rendered him no less unsightly than treacherous. If all men signalized by virtue are fully developed in their moral organs now, there is good reason to believe that the same law will be in force during that more felicitous period when peace and concord shall every where prevail, and righteousness and piety cover the earth. In the mean time, it will not be denied, that it is our duty, both as moralists and Christians, to make, by human means, as near an approach as practicable to millennial perfection. And an approach of great value to our race *can* be made by a well-concerted and well-administered scheme of education. Progress in virtue and morality is as much the result of practical and proper training, as dexterous horsemanship, or skill in arms. By suitable measures, the former is as easily and certainly attainable as the latter.

Is any one inclined to propose the question, " Can the organs of the brain be *increased in size*, as well as rendered more adroit and vigorous in action, by any process of training?" I answer, Yes, with as much certainty as the muscles of the extremities can be increased in size, provided the process be commenced in childhood. On this principle depends the perfectibility of man; I mean his susceptibility of the highest improvement compatible with the laws imposed on his nature. Abrogate the principle, and his case is hopeless.

Take two children, of the same sex and age, formed and organized as nearly alike as possible. Educate one skilfully, and the other unskilfully; or do not educate the latter at all; and, by the time of their maturity, they will differ in figure, size, organization, and faculties. And each point of difference will prove the power and the advantage of education. Have the lower extremities of the one been exercised in walking, running, and leaping, much more than those of the other? They will be larger and more powerful, and much less easily exhausted by fatigue. Have the hands and arms been the subjects of training? They will surpass the untrained ones in bulk and strength. Has the brain of one of the individuals been exercised more than that of the other? The same will be true of it. Its size, figure, and force will be augmented. Has the animal compartment of one party been highly excited and fed by vicious indulgences, and the moral compartment of the other been equally trained in sentiments leading to practical virtue? Here will be ground for another difference. In the latter, the moral organs will be enlarged, and the animal diminished, at least comparatively; while, in the former, the reverse will occur—the animal compartment will be augmented at the expense of the moral. Cultivate the knowing and reflecting compartment, to the neglect of the other two, and in it will be the increase in size and vigour. Thus, as relates to augmentation and diminution, power and weakness, the brain is governed by the same laws with other portions of organic matter. I do not say that it can be increased in bulk by exercise, as much as muscles, but it can as certainly.

Another principle of great importance invites our attention. Other things being equal, in proportion to the size of either compartment of the brain, is its proneness to action, and the gratification which that action bestows on the individual. Does the animal compartment preponderate? The taste for animal indulgences is keen, the pleasure derived from them intense, and the danger of lawless devotion to them great. Does the moral compartment surpass in size? A wish to comply with moral obligation constitutes the ruling passion of the party thus organized, and his chief delight is to do his duty. To him each act of well-doing is its own reward. He "follows virtue even for virtue's sake." This he does from *moral instinct*, without the influence of human laws, or any positive divine command. The law he obeys is that of his own constitution. He has a law in himself. The person whose intellectual department predominates, is devoted to inquiry, if not to study. He delights in knowledge, deems it a valuable possession, and devises and practises some mode of attaining it. The kind of knowledge most agreeable to him is determined by the intellectual organs most developed.

As relates to education and the improvement it produces, these views are important and encouraging. They point out a plain and easy process by which the condition of man may be improved. If the moral and intellectual compartments of a child be small, they may be enlarged by training; and in proportion as they grow will its taste for knowledge and virtue increase. By maturity in years this taste will be confirmed, and, in organization and its effects, the amended condition of the adult will surpass not a little the promise of the child. By the law of inheritance heretofore referred to, the children of this individual, resembling himself in his mature condition, will be better organized than he was in his childhood. Train them and their descendants as he was trained, and organic improvement will go on in them, until in time the highest perfection of their nature shall be attained. Extend this treatment to the whole human race, and universal improvement in organization will be the issue. Then will be completed, on grounds that nothing can shake, the triumph of the intellectual and moral over the animal character of man.

Am I asked in what way the moral compartment of the brain is to be cultivated, strengthened, and enlarged? I answer, by all sorts of moral excitement; inculcating moral precepts, presenting moral examples, eliciting moral sentiments, but more especially by associating with companions strictly moral, and engaging early in the moral practice of doing good. Reading the biographies of men remarkable for high and practical morality, and well-written works of moral fiction, contributes materially to the same end. This course, skilfully and inflexibly pursued, will infallibly strengthen and enlarge the moral organs, and confirm those persons subjected to its influence in habits of virtue.

The perfect physical education of the brain consists in the competent exercise of every portion of it; so that each of its organs may possess due strength and activity and be itself healthy, and that there may exist between them the equilibrium necessary to the health and regulated action of the whole. If one or more organs be exercised too much, they may become exhausted and debilitated, or excited to inflammation, or a condition bordering on it and not less truly morbid; while others, being exercised too little or not at all, will be enfeebled by inaction. And thus must the health, not only of the brain, but of the whole system, suffer; for I have already observed, and need scarcely repeat, that the brain, being one of the ruling viscera of the system, any derangement of it must injure the condition of all the others. I shall only add, that cerebral organs are prone to become exhausted, or inflamed, according to their character. Are they small, phlegmatic, and feeble? severe exercise prostrates them. Are they large, high-toned, and vigorous? intense exercise inflames them, or produces in them such irritability and inordinate action, as derange the balance of the brain, excite mental irregularities, and lay the foundation of cerebral disease.

This view of the subject shews the propriety and advantage of pupils pursuing several studies, or modes of mental exercise, at the same time, instead of being confined exclusively to one. It suggests, moreover, the reason of it. By changing from one study to another successively, in the same day, those who are cultivating science and letters not only learn much more than they could under confinement to a single study, but do so with less exhaustion and danger to health. Why? Because, by closely studying one branch of knowledge only—in other words, by labouring all day with one cerebral organ—it becomes exhausted and dull, as every industrious student must have felt. When thus worn out, therefore, by toil, not only is it unfit to exercise further with due effect, and master its task; but its health is endangered, if not, for the time, actually injured. It is in a fatigued condition, which borders on a diseased one, and often excites it. When, on the contrary, the pupil, feeling himself becoming unfit for one study, passes to another, he engages in the latter with a fresh and active organ, and makes rapid progress in it, until, beginning to be again fatigued and dull, he changes to a third, or returns to that previously relinquished, the organ corresponding to it being reinvigorated by rest. To illustrate my views, by examples familiar to every individual who has received an education :—

If the pupil begin the study of language, say of Greek or Latin, in the morning, and continue it during the whole day, he will be so toilworn and dull by night, as to be scarcely able to distinguish a noun from a verb.

But if, instead of this injudicious and unprofitable course, he pursue the study of language two or three hours, then pass to mathematics, and next to geography or history, continuing each form of exercise a reasonable time—by thus changing the working organs, and allowing them alternately to refresh themselves by rest, he may study with equal intenseness, and an equal number of hours in the day,—and, by night, feeling little or no fatigue, have acquired much more knowledge, at a less risk of health, than he could have done by the protracted toil of a single organ. Independently of the attainment made in history and geography, he will have a clearer and better knowledge even of his task in language than he would have acquired had he brooded over it during the whole day. Shifting the toil, in this manner, from one organ to another, is like bringing fresh soldiers into battle to relieve their exhausted comrades, or hands not yet fatigued to the labours of the harvest-field. By such changes, judiciously made, success is achieved; while any other mode of proceeding would result in failure.*

* Change from one study to another, even where both fall within the province of the same faculty, is refreshing and beneficial; just as appetite for food is revived by a change of dishes. It is always better, however, to bring, if possible, a different organ into play. The following remarks by Dr Kirkpatrick on this subject deserve to be quoted. "A recourse to such musical airs as are most agreeable to the ear of a person fatigued with long and intense study, might prove recreating and useful, by exciting the action of different nerves from those which have been over-exercised by long thought and attention, and which must have need of rest. I am acquainted with a sedentary person, greatly addicted to reading, who assures me, that when he has found himself nearly stupified by attending to one book or subject, he has found his apprehension sufficiently awake on recurring directly to a different one. Another gentleman, of considerable application to various reading, also informs me, that when he has read himself into a headach and a sensible obtuseness of distinguishing, an immediate diversion to elegant poetical works, or even to writing a little poetry, for which he is thought to have some talent, has entirely removed his headach, and proved as sensibly cordial to him as he supposes music would have been to a person of a better musical ear than his own. These observations naturally remind me of that circumstance in the pagan mythology, which ascribes the powers of medicine, of poetry, and of music, to the same heathen deity, Apollo."—R. C.

Connected with this topic are two points on which I am anxious to fix your attention, because I consider them peculiarly important. Much of their importance, moreover, arises from their being exclusively practical; and from the further fact, that serious and even fatal errors in relation to them are often committed.

That I may be the more easily and perfectly understood, I shall repeat what has been already stated, that very weak and dull organs, and very powerful and active ones, are differently affected by excessive exercise. The former are prostrated and rendered unfit for action, as a feeble and phlegmatic man is by danger and oppression; while, like a brave and powerful man of a fiery temperament, the latter are roused to high excitement, and perhaps inflammation. Occurrences in illustration and proof of this are not unfrequent in seats of learning.

Parents or guardians resolve that a youth, whose organs of Language, Size, and Number are small and feeble, shall, notwithstanding, be made a linguist and a mathematician. To effect this, the pupil is compelled, or in some way induced, to labour to excess, with his feeble organs, which are easily worn out, until the exhaustion and injury they have sustained prove prejudicial and perhaps ruinous to his other organs, which are of a better cast, as well as to his general health. Fatuity and insanity have been thus brought on. Again, another pupil has the same organs in fine development, and highly excitable, active, and vigorous. His talents for language and mathematics are discovered to be of the first order, and both he and his friends are ambitious that he should excel in the knowledge of them. Hence he is encouraged and incited to pursue the study of them, with such ardour and perseverance, as to produce in the organs exercised a state of intense and morbid irritation, and perhaps inflammation. By this imprudent excitement, madness and phrenitis, with other grievous maladies of the brain, have been repeatedly induced. Of the indiscreet and excessive exercise of other strong and feeble organs, whether animal, moral, or intellectual, the same is true.

Is any one inclined to ask me, how he is to know when a youth possesses weak, and when strong organs, for particular studies? The answer is easy. The practical phrenologist makes the discovery by virtue of his art, and is rarely mistaken. Dr Spurzheim did this in Boston in scores of instances, to the surprise and delight of many of the most enlightened inhabitants of the place; and in Edinburgh, London, Dublin, and Paris, and other parts of Great Britain and France, the practice has become so common that it surprises no longer. There being, however, unfortunately but few practical phrenologists in our country, those who are not so may, from the following considerations, derive some portion of the knowledge desired. Every one takes pleasure in the exercise of his well-developed and vigorous organs, and exerts them with good effect; and the reverse. The exercise of his feeble ones is a matter of indifference, if not dissatisfaction to him; and he makes but little progress in any study in which they are chiefly concerned. Has a pupil, for example, a predominant taste for language, music, painting, and mechanical handicraft, or either of them? and does he make attainments in them with ease and rapidity? his organs and faculties for them are good. Is the reverse of this the case? his organs for them are feeble. The practical precept deducible from this statement is plain. Never urge a pupil to an excessive exertion of feeble cerebral organs, it being both useless and dangerous—useless, because he can in no way become respectable himself, or render high services to others by them; and dangerous, because it may impair his intellect and destroy his health. For the same reason, do not encourage or permit a youth to persevere to excess in the exercise of highly sensitive and vigorous organs. The practice is like exposing an irritable or an inflamed eye to a glare of light, or assailing a phrenitic brain with piercing sounds. By a strict observance of these precepts in seats of education, much time might be saved which is now wasted, much evil prevented, and much good done. The necessity of their enforcement is strengthened by the fact, that children and youth of precocious and large developments, and unusually active and vigorous talents, possess, in general, delicate and sometimes feeble constitutions. Their systems are therefore the more easily deranged, and should be guarded with the greater care.

From the preceding facts, another important precept may be drawn. Of a boy whose whole brain is unusually small, never attempt to make a scholar, a professional character, or a man of science. The effort will not only eventuate in failure, but may prove ruinous to health. In a particular manner, it may induce fatuity, should the feeble-brained individual become severely studious. As well might you attempt to convert a dwarf into a grenadier, as a person with a very small head into a man of a powerful and expanded intellect. Nor would it be less vain to endeavour to imbue with learning or science a boy whose brain is unusually large in the animal compartment, and small in the intellectual and moral ones. Such an individual is formed by nature for a low sphere of mind, and no effort in education can elevate him. Nor, could any training render him studious, would he be less liable to some kind of mental alienation than the youth whose entire brain is small. Individuals thus organized may become great animals, and may even perform striking and impressive actions; but they can never attain rank as men of intellect. In war, they may be brave and useful soldiers and inferior officers, but must be totally incompetent to high command.*

---

* It was a favourite maxim with Sir William Jones, that no intellectual eminence which had ever been reached by one man was unattainable by any other. Such an opinion is well calculated to stimulate young men to industry and exertion, and, if acted upon, may sometimes in this way lead to beneficial results; but, at the same time, it is obvious, that of those who proceed on the supposition that a lofty pinnacle of intellectual greatness is within their reach, a vast majority must necessarily find a bitter disappointment of their hopes. Sir William Jones was a man of extraordinary natural talent, and fell into the grave error of supposing every man to be endowed with abilities equal to his

Does any one doubt, whether the moral organs and faculties can be exercised, and moral feelings indulged in, to excess? and whether, in physical education, they ought to be in any cases restrained? Is it, on the contrary, the belief, that the more high-toned every thing belonging to our moral nature is, its perfection is the greater? Let all doubt and delusion on these points be removed, by the recollection that the organ of Benevolence becomes, by inordinate excitement, so far deranged, in many persons, as to induce them to squander their estates, to the ruin of themselves and their families, in wild and unprofitable charities, and other acts of morbid generosity; while, by the ultra-excitement of Veneration, Hope, and Wonder, others become religiously insane. Castle-building, running into mental derangement, as it often does,

own. Nobody will deny that an idiot is incapable of attaining eminence in any intellectual pursuit; and observation shews that there is a regular gradation of minds from idiocy up to the genius of a Newton, a Franklin, or a Locke. If a person of moderate talent engages in a study too deep for his limited powers, under the idea that, by dint of application, he is sure to master it in the end, the forced and constrained exertion infallibly proves injurious to his health and destructive of mental tranquillity. "It appears to me very singular," says Hufeland, "that when it is requisite to raise up a corporeal burden, people always first try it by their strength, to discover whether it be not too heavy for them; but in regard to a mental burden, never consult their powers to know whether they are sufficient to sustain it. How many have I seen miserable and enervated, merely because they attempted to dive to the depths of philosophy without having philosophical heads! Must every man, then, be a philosopher by profession, as seems to be the mode at present? In my opinion, a particular organization is necessary for that purpose; and it may be left to the chosen few to investigate and unfold the secrets of philosophy: as to others, let them be contented with *acting* and *living* like philosophers."—(*Art of Prolonging Human Life*, part 2, ch. 3.) The same remarks are applicable to those who, without the requisite qualifications, assume the charge of difficult and complicated affairs in mercantile life. They find themselves out of harmony with their employment, are bewildered and perplexed amid a concourse of urgent duties, and, finally, either become bankrupt, or retire with gladness to a more contracted sphere, the occupations of which are suited to their abilities and tastes.—R. C.

is likewise the product of inordinate action in moral organs.* Go to a mad-house, and you will find fiery and vociferous religious insanity one of the common affections of its inmates.† Every leaning of this sort, inordinately strong, should be moderated in children by some form of counter excitement—I mean, by giving, as far as possible, the feelings and thoughts a different direction. Yet the practice is too often the reverse of this. The youthful are encouraged in their enthusiastic devotions, until madness strikes them. Hence, on every occurrence of a new sect or denomination in religion, as well as in most cases of what are called *revivals*, religious enthusiasm effervesces, in many instances, into wild insanity. That there is much madness among the new sects of Mormonites and Immortalists, no one can doubt. The cause is, ultra-excitement in some portion of the moral compartment of the brain. Even the sentiment of Conscientiousness may run to excess, and become productive of unreasonable scrupulousness and demur.

The great end of the physical education of the brain, as already intimated, is to strengthen the whole of it, and maintain a due balance among its several parts. What is commonly called *eccentricity, brown study*, or *absence of mind*, is but another name for a want of such balance, and is a true and dangerous bent towards madness. Augment it to a sufficient extent—in other words, excite sufficiently the irregular and extravagant organ—and real madness is the result. Hence, most persons who become insane, especially those who fall into hereditary insanity, exhibit in their characters, even from childhood, some

* This is true, on the supposition that the faculty of Hope is a moral sentiment; which, however, does not seem to be the fact. See the Note on p. 63.—R. C.

† Numerous cases of this kind of insanity are reported in the ninth volume of the Phrenological Journal, in a series of very instructive articles, entitled " Observations on Religious Fanaticism; illustrated by a comparison of the belief and conduct of noted religious enthusiasts with those of patients in the Montrose Lunatic Asylum. By W. A. F. Browne, Esq. Medical Superintendent of that Institution."—R. C.

uncommon and ominous traits—something that is called *eccentric* or *queer*. In proof of this, the histories of the tenants of lunatic hospitals furnish abundant testimony. They shew that a large majority of those unfortunate individuals had been more or less eccentric. The evil consists in a state of supra-excitement and action in some of the cerebral organs. And physical education alone can remedy it. Take the following anecdote as an illustration of my meaning. A gentleman of Philadelphia, highly distinguished for his talents and standing, was subject to fits of extraordinary absence of mind—in other words, to such entire absorption in the working of one or two of the cerebral organs, as to be insensible to that of all the others. He once invited a large number of his friends to dinner. On the day appointed, the guests assembled in his drawing-room, where he met them with his usual welcome and courtesy, and conversed with them with his accustomed sprightliness and good sense. He became at length silent and abstracted, mused for a minute or two, and then bowing to the company, begged them to excuse him, as he had an urgent piece of business to transact immediately. One of the gentlemen, well acquainted with the irregularity of his mind, addressing him familiarly by his christian name, asked him, " Did you not invite us to dine with you to-day ?"—" Did I ?" said he, " perhaps so ; I'll see." He stepped into his dining-room, where a table was sumptuously spread for him and his friends. Returning to the company, he joined them, first in merriment at his absent fit, and then in the pleasures of the repast. The sequel is melancholy. He became deranged in his mind, and died in that condition in the Pennsylvania hospital.

As already suggested, the cure of this evil is to be performed by giving rest to the over-active cerebral organs, and transferring the excitement to some of the others that are less irritable. Phrenology teaches the mode of conducting this process, on which a want of time forbids me to dilate. Permit me, however, to observe, that its power to weaken, and, by its continued operation through successive generations, ultimately eradicate, a hereditary predisposition to madness, gives physical education much of its value. A predisposition to madness consists in faulty organization, at least in a condition of the brain destitute of soundness. But the fault has not existed through all generations. It had a beginning, and that beginning was the product of a series of deleterious impressions. Another series of counter-impressions, therefore, may remove the mischief. Changes thus produced, may thus be done away. Of this no reasonable doubt can be entertained. Daily occurrences convince us of its truth. Every thing indeed that bears on it testifies to that effect. No one has ever yet been predisposed to madness in every organ of his brain. The mischief is always local; often, perhaps generally, confined at first to a single organ. Let its seat be ascertained (and the ascertainment is practicable) and proper training will in time remove it. But the process must be commenced in childhood. Should it fail to eradicate entirely the predisposition from the son or daughter of the insane, it will at least weaken it. In his grandchildren it will further weaken it, and in a future generation completely efface it. But to attain the end, the means must be skilfully and steadily applied. Am I asked for a recital of them? I reply, that they must differ in different cases; and time does not permit me to refer to any of them. The enlightened phrenologist will have no difficulty in discovering and employing them. And none but a phrenologist can have a just conception of the philosophy, prevention, or treatment of madness. Nor ought any other to pretend to them. As well may a tyro, who never witnessed a dissection, or listened to a lecture on anatomy, attempt the most difficult operation in surgery.

But if the brain be thus changed and amended by education, may not similar benefits be extended on similar principles to other organs?—to the lungs and the chylopoetic viscera? Unquestionably they may; and thus may predisposition to pulmonary consumption, gout, dyspepsia, scrofula, and all other maladies transmitted by ancestors, be removed from posterity. The enfeebled organ may be strengthened and placed on a par with the others, and thus the balance of the system may be restored. But here again the preventive treatment must begin in childhood, and be steadily persevered in, if not to the close of life, at least to an advanced period in its decline. In a few generations such procedure cannot fail to eradicate the evil. It is believed that, if skilfully and perseveringly applied, the remedy is competent to the end contemplated. Thus may hereditary disease be effaced. The vices, follies, and misfortunes of ancestors will be no longer visited on an amended posterity.

In fact, physical education, hitherto so much neglected, and still so imperfectly understood and practised, may be pronounced the ARBITER of the human mind, no less than of the human body. Its influence in strengthening or weakening, improving or deteriorating, all kinds of mental faculties and operations, is far greater than is commonly imagined. Through its instrumentality alone can man attain, in mind as well as body, the highest perfection of which he is susceptible. It is destined, therefore, as heretofore observed, to be the chief agent in the production of the millennium, at whatever period that improved condition of our race may occur. This is as certain as it is, that a well-directed physical education is the principal means to improve, to the highest pitch, the qualities of our domestic animals. And that truth will not be controverted.

Let it never be forgotten, then, that the physical education of the human race ought not to be confined alone to the humble object of preventing disease. Its aim should be loftier and more in accordance with the destiny and character of its subject—to raise man to the summit of his nature. And such will be its scope in future and more enlightened ages.

In saying that to promote and secure the health of the human system, the brain should be educated and amended, I mean, as already intimated, the whole brain; its animal and moral, as well as its intellectual compartments.

It is only by a general and judicious training, that the proper equilibrium between the cerebral organs can be established and maintained. And that equilibrium is as necessary to the sound condition of the whole body, as to that of the brain itself. It produces an equipoise of the entire man, and holds in check the irregularities and excesses of both feeling and action, which prey on life, and tend to shorten it. Hence long-lived individuals have usually possessed a marked calmness and equability of character. Why? Because their brains have been well balanced. If their feelings were strong, so were their powers to control them. Men of a burning temper and boisterous disposition, who are perpetually running into extremes, and who pass much of their time between sinning and repenting, rarely attain to a very advanced age. The reason is obvious. Their health and strength are consumed in their own fires; and those fires come from the brain—I mean its animal compartment. That portion is the seat of what is usually termed *passion*, which, when fierce and unrestrained, resembles intemperance in the use of strong drink. It inflames or otherwise deranges the brain, hastens the approach of old age, and curtails life, on the same principles. In delicate and irritable systems, it often excites convulsions, and sometimes palsy, apoplexy, and madness.

The following facts testify to the truth of the principles just laid down. The life of women is more secure than that of men. In other words, fewer of them die in a given period. In each census of the British empire, the number of women is found to be greater than that of men. Yet there are more males than females born in the empire, in the proportion of 105 to 100. Though war, casualty, migration and death in foreign and sickly countries, account for this in part, they are insufficient for the solution of the entire problem. The greater strength, more frequent and unrestrained bursts, and more constant burning of the passions of men, contribute to the event.

Again. The less impassionate the pursuits of men of genius are, the greater is the average longevity of each class of them. Mathematicians and natural philosophers have but little in their studies to excite feeling or stir up passion. The *tenor* of their lives is generally tranquil. Hence the aggregate age of twenty of them, taken promiscuously, has been found to amount to 1504 years, giving to each the average of 75.

Poets, on the contrary, are proverbially an '*irritabile genus*,'—men of strong and easily excited feelings, and a burning imagination. Their productions, moreover, being works of passion, their minds must be in tumult during their composition. From these causes, the aggregate age of twenty distinguished poets has been ascertained to be 1144 years, giving to each an average of 57—a very striking balance in favour of a mind free from passion!

In our efforts to produce an equipoise in the brain, one fact should be held in remembrance, and observed as a leading ground of action. By nature, the animal organs are larger and more powerful than the moral or intellectual. This is the case in every one, but in some individuals much more strikingly so than in others. It is true of man, therefore, that he posseses naturally more of animality than of real humanity. Hence the comparative ferocity and savageism of the uneducated. Why? Because their animal organs, never having been restrained and tamed, predominate greatly over their moral and intellectual, more especially over the reflective ones. This constitutes the chief difference between the cultivated and the uncultivated portions of our race. The latter are more of animals, the former more of men.

This view of the subject indicates clearly the leading purpose of the physical education of the brain. It is to strengthen the moral and intellectual organs, by exciting them to action, each in a manner corresponding to its nature, and to weaken *comparatively* the animal organs, by restraining their action.* Thus will the former at-

* It is hardly necessary to remark, that the process here recommended ought to be reversed in cases where a too small endowment of

tain, by degrees, such an ascendency over the latter, as to be able to control them, and give calmness and equability to the character of the individual—to convert the rude animal into the cultivated man. Nor is the condition of the brain thus produced less friendly to the welfare of the body, than to the sound operations of the mind.

The influence of strong and well-cultivated moral and intellectual organs on the general health of the system is soothing and salutary, and feeds and strengthens it, instead of ruffling and wearing it out. Compared to the influence of the organs of passion, it is as mild and wholesome nourishment, contrasted with alcohol; or like the genial warmth of the spring and autumn, with the burning heats of summer. Life, and health, and comfort may last long under the former, while all is parched and withered by the latter. Finally, a well-cultivated and well-balanced brain does much to produce and maintain a sound mind in a sound body. Let the attainment of it, therefore, be a leading aim in physical education.

Of innumerable instances that might be cited in proof of the principle here contended for, I shall refer to but one; and that is memorable in the history of our country. The Declaration of Independence was signed by fifty-six delegates, all of them men of well-cultivated and well-balanced minds. In other words, their moral and intellectual had gained the requisite ascendency over their animal organs. Of these, two died of casualties, in the prime of manhood. The aggregate of the years of the other fifty-four was 3609, giving to each an average of sixty-six years and nine months; an illustrious example of the influence of well-cultivated and regulated brains, in conferring longevity on those who possess them. Several of these great and good men lived beyond their

---

the animal organs is possessed. Individuals in whom the propensities are very weak, experience much difficulty in keeping their ground in society; they want boldness and the requisite disposition to attend to self-interest, and are rendered unhappy by the wide-spreading misery and injustice which they see around them.—R. C.

eightieth year, and some of them passed the age of ninety. It is not to be doubted that the avoidance of all forms of excess, and the general correctness of the habits produced by this condition of the brain, contributes materially to the prolongation of life. The venerable Madison, of a feeble frame, possesses one of the best cultivated and balanced minds that ever existed, and he is now (1833) in his eighty-fifth year.

The importance of the judicious education and general management of the brain, and the serious evils arising from neglect and errors in them, lead me, though somewhat out of my immediate track, to make a few further remarks on the subject. My sense of duty, and therefore my ruling motive to this effect, is the stronger, in consideration of the fact, that the thoughts I have to offer apply more forcibly to our own country than to any other.

Dyspepsia and mental derangement are among the most grievous maladies that affect the human race; and they are much more nearly allied to each other than they are generally supposed to be. So true is this, that the one is not unfrequently converted into the other, and often alternates with it. The lunatic is usually a dyspeptic during his lucid intervals; and complaints which begin in some form of gastric derangement, turn, in many instances, to madness. Nor is this all. In families where mental derangement is hereditary, the members who escape that complaint are more than usually obnoxious to dyspepsia. It may be added, that dyspeptics and lunatics are relieved by the same modes of treatment, and that their maladies are induced, for the most part, by the same causes.

Somewhat in confirmation of these views, it may be further stated, that dyspepsia and madness prevail more extensively in the United States, in proportion to the number of our inhabitants, than among the people of any other nation. Of the amount of our dyspeptics no estimate can be formed; but it is immense. Whether we inquire in cities, towns, villages, or country places—among the rich, the poor, or those in moderate circumstances—we find dyspepsia more or less prevalent throughout the land. In other countries, this is not the case—not, I mean, to any thing near the same extent. True, in Great Britain, Germany, and France, the complaint assails the higher classes of society; but there it stops,—the common and lower classes scarcely knowing it, except by name. In Italy, Spain, and Portugal, it is still less common among all ranks of the people. The apparent cause of these things will be referred to presently.

Insanity prevails in our country to an alarming extent, and, in common with dyspepsia, is on the increase. The entire number of the insane, in the United States, is computed at *fifty thousand*—a most startling aggregate, and, I trust, beyond the *real* one: yet the real one, were it ascertained, would be very great; sufficient to excite strict inquiries into the cause, accompanied by strenuous efforts for its removal. According to a late and very intelligent writer,* whose information and accuracy deserve our confidence, there are *a thousand* lunatics in the State of Connecticut. This is in the ratio of *one* to every *two hundred and sixty-two* of the inhabitants of the State. In England, the number of insane persons does not exceed *twelve* or *thirteen* thousand. In the agricultural districts there, the average ratio is about *one in eight hundred and twenty* of the whole population, being to that of Connecticut less than one to three. Yet in England the disease prevails to a greater extent than in any other nation of Europe. In Scotland, the general proportion, including towns and cities as well as country places, is *one in five hundred and seventy-four*.† There is every where more madness, according to the amount of population, in cities than in the country. In Spain and Russia, the large cities excepted, there is very

* Dr Brigham.

† These statements cannot be held as more than approximating the truth. Hitherto the statistics of insanity have been so much neglected, that accurate information is unattainable. Nor is it easy to see that circumstances will in this respect suffer a change, unless comprehensive inquiries be set on foot by Government.—R.C.

little; in Turkey, Persia, and China, still less. Of Hindostan I believe the same is true; and in savage nations, especially where no ardent spirits are used, the complaint is scarcely known. Such is the report of all travellers among the Indians of North and South America. To this it may be subjoined, that the insanity of a people is increased by the occurrence among them of any deep and extensive mental commotion, whether from theological or political causes. Such, as history informs us, was the effect of the Reformation by Luther, of the Revolution by Cromwell, of the American Revolution, and more especially of the first Revolution in France. During the convulsions of the latter event, the frequency of insanity in Paris was frightful.

From these facts it appears, that in proportion to the freedom of action of the human mind in any country, more especially in proportion as it is tossed and perplexed by strong passions and emotions, is the amount of madness by which that country is visited. This result we should expect, from calculation on well-known principles; and observation testifies to its truth. In common times, there is more mental agitation in Great Britain than in France; more in France than in Spain or Russia; and much more in either of them than in Turkey, Persia, or China. And in savage tribes, except during the hours of hunting and battle, there is no mental agitation at all—none certainly of a *distracting* character. The causes of these several facts are plain. It clearly appears that, in civilized nations, the degree of distracting mental emotion which the people generally experience, is in proportion to the amount of the freedom they enjoy; and that again depends on the more or less popular characters of their governments. The people of England and Scotland enjoy more freedom than the people of France; and the latter more than those of Spain or Russia. In Turkey, Persia, and China, political freedom is unknown. The despotism of government compresses the minds of the subjects into a dead and hopeless calm. Unable to render their condition any better, the degraded population cease, in appearance, to wish it so, or even to disquiet themselves by a thought on the subject.

Very different is the condition of things in the United States. Our freedom, both political and religious, is ample; and we push and enjoy it to its utmost limits. Our institutions, moreover, of every description, are as popular as comports with social order and sound government. State and church preferment and office are open to every one; and the ardour, keenness, and constancy of competition and struggle for them, have no example in the practices of the present, or the history of the past. The fervour and commotion of electioneering intrigue has no respite. Under such form, the country is agitated, I might almost say convulsed, by it, from the beginning to the end of the year, and of every year. Thus are the angry and burning passions kept for ever awake among the people, and often urged to the most intense action. My present allusion is chiefly to the interminable and embittered war of party-politics.

Of party-religion nearly the same is true. Sectarian embroilment, battle, and intrigue, are constant, furious, and vengeful. Sometimes the strife is about a doctrinal tenet, at other times about a formal rite or ceremony, and again for the achievement of power and influence; one sect struggling for the mastery over the rest, at least to outstrip them in schemes of ambition. Nor must I forget the fervid and unceasing labours of the pastor and preacher for the conversion and edification of his flock, and the wild and convulsive emotion he often produces in their minds. In no other nation are these several forms of excitement half so high and agitating as in the United States. A similar condition of things exists in the congregation of the celebrated Irving of London, many of whose hearers are occasionally deranged.

Another source of deep disquietude to the inhabitants of our country, is the desire and pursuit of wealth. A more ardently money-loving and keenly money-seeking people than the Americans does not exist. I doubt much whether, in these respects, any equals them. The reason of this is plain. The nature of our government and of all our institutions encourages and urges every one to aim at standing and power; and the possession of wealth aids greatly in the attainment of them. Indeed, hereditary titles and standing being unknown to us, the only actual elements of rank and power in the United States are wealth and place. Without these, talents however splendid, and knowledge however varied and extensive, give to their possessor but little influence. Nor is this all. Owing to our youthful and unsettled character as a people, the modes of acquiring wealth are not so well established in the United States as in the countries of Europe. Business does not run in so regular a channel. There is more of random traffic and speculation in it; and these forms of transacting it, being often suddenly productive of great profit, and at other times of ruinous losses, and keeping the mind constantly on the stretch of the calculation of chances, are much more exciting and harassing than they would be were they more uniform and certain. Men engaged in regular and well-settled business pursue it mechanically, are calm during the day, and sleep soundly at night. But dealers and speculators, besides being constantly disquieted while awake, are tossed between sudden wealth and ruin in their dreams. They are equally distracted by the uncertainty and the unexpected occurrence of events.

Such are the three leading sources of mental commotion in our country—party-politics, party-religion, and the love of wealth. Nor is it to be doubted, that they produce in the minds of the people a greater amount of harassing and giddy excitement than exists, perhaps, in all other nations united. But mental excitement is only another name for cerebral excitement. Nor must it be forgotten that the early mismanagement and debilitating practice of over-working the brains of children, in infant and other early schools, disqualify them to maintain their soundness, in after life, under a degree of irritation which they might have otherwise sustained without much injury. If the lungs be injured and weakened in infancy or childhood, no one doubts that the individual thus affected will be more than usually liable to pulmonary complaints. Why? Because the lungs are not only more susceptible of malign impressions, but less able to resist them and escape the mischief they are calculated to produce. Of the brain, the same is true. If it be weakened in childhood, it will be afterwards inordinately liable to morbid affections, and too feeble to contend with them.

That these causes contribute to the production of the inordinate sum of insanity which prevails in the United States, is too plain to be held in doubt; for madness is the result of cerebral excitement, rendered deleterious by the excess in quantity, or the malign qualities, of the irritants that produce it. Nor can any cerebral irritant be more noxious, either in kind or degree, than the cankered and fierce religious and political passions which are constantly goading the American brain. Under such circumstances, it would be wonderful if attacks of insanity were not unusually frequent among us.

But can the same causes prove also instrumental in the production of dyspepsia?—No doubt of it. That complaint *commences*, perhaps, as often in the brain as in the stomach—possibly oftener. That this is true of the disease in Europe, will scarcely be denied, after a fair examination of the facts connected with it. It is there, almost exclusively, a complaint of the studious and the scheming, who, over-tasking their brains, injure them by toil. Among the husbandmen of England, who steadily pursue their tranquil mode of life, regardless of the fluctuations of stock, the bickerings of party, the fate of political measures, and the changes of place, dyspepsia is almost a stranger. Yet many of those men are great eaters, and far from being very choice as to the quality of their food. In the cities, the same is in a great measure true of merchants, manufacturers, and mechanics, who are engaged in a regular and well-established business, which is fully understood by them, where the risk is slight and the profits sure, and no disquieting anxiety attends it. Such individuals have a good digestion, and bear the marks of it. But, with literary men, officers of state, dealers in scrip, daring adventurers and anxious and ambitious projectors of improvements,—with these, and every other brain-worn class of persons, the case is different. Dyspepsia is their torment; and they exhibit deep traces of it, in their lean frames and haggard countenances. Yet are they much more select in their diet, both as respects quantity, quality, and cooking, than the classes to whom dyspepsia is unknown. This fact is notorious, and has been so for centuries. Nor can it be attributed, I think, to any other cause but excessive and deleterious cerebral irritation in the one case, and an exemption from it in the other. And this cause seems sufficient to solve the problem.

That it is not exclusively the labour and irritation of the stomach that produces dyspepsia, appears from innumerable other facts, a few of which I shall recite. Children not too much confined in school, or otherwise mistreated, though great and often promiscuous eaters, are rarely dyspeptic. The reason is plain. Their brains are neither toil-worn nor care-worn, and they enjoy the requisite amount of sleep. Their brains are not irritated and exhausted by burdensome tasks. The North American Indians eat at times enormously, and that after a *long fast*, which, on well-known principles, increases the danger of overloading the stomach. It is said that, on these occasions, the meal of a single Indian is equal to that of from four to six white men. The food, moreover, is badly cooked, and therefore indigestible. Yet the savage escapes dyspepsia.

Of the Esquimaux Indians the same is true to a still greater extent. An individual of that tribe, as we are confidently assured by Captain Parry and Captain Lyon, eats with impunity from ten to twelve pounds of solid animal food in the course of a day, and swallows along with it, in the form of drink, a gallon of oil. Captain Lyon further relates, that a young female Esquimaux ate a large amount of candles and their wicks, without sustaining either sickness or dyspepsia. These statements we are compelled to believe, on account of the high respectability of the authors of them.*

Of the gluttony of the Siberians stories are told, not perhaps altogether so worthy of credit. Were not that people, however, enormous eaters, such stories would not be invented. The accounts are but exaggerations of extraordinary gormandizing. It is asserted by travellers, that a Siberian often eats in a day *forty pounds* of solid food; and Admiral Saritchaff reports, that he saw one of that people eat, *immediately after breakfast,* twenty-five pounds of boiled rice and *three pounds* of butter. Yet, as already stated, neither Siberians nor Esquimaux are annoyed by dyspepsia; and they, no doubt, owe their safety, in part, to their freedom from wasting cerebral irritation.

For the same reason the inferior animals have no dyspepsia, though they often gorge themselves to great excess. When they thus violate moderation, nature teaches them what to do for safety. They instinctively lie down and sleep, giving entire freedom and rest to their brains. A common black snake swallows a rabbit or a squirrel nearly as weighty as itself, and goes into a partial torpor until its meal is digested. A boa-constrictor swallows a goat or an antelope, sleeps nearly a week, and wakes without dyspepsia or uneasiness, prepared for another similar exploit. Two dogs of the same age, size, and strength, having eaten the same amount of the same food, one of them goes to sleep, and the other enters on the

* An amusing illustration is narrated by Captain Lyon. A lamp having been purchased by Captain Parry while it was burning, "the woman who sold it instantly extinguished the light, and vigorously commenced cleaning the lamp, which contained as much soot as oil, by scraping it with her fingers, which, with their load of sweets, she conveyed rapidly to her mouth. The tongue finished the operation; the lamp was licked perfectly clean, while, in return, it covered her face with soot, and caused us all a laugh at her uncouth figure, in which she joined most heartily."—Lyon's *Private Journal*, p. 119.— R. C.

chase. In from three to four hours the meal of the sleeper is digested, while that of the runner is unchanged in his stomach—and the latter dog is probably disordered, while the former retains his health. These facts shew that tranquillity of the brain is favourable at least, if not essential, to the process of easy and sound digestion.

The powerful influence of a disordered brain over the digestive system, is manifested in the effects of a severe blow on the head. These are vomiting, gastric inflammation, hepatic derangement, amounting at times to abscess, and again to torpor of the liver, with other forms of abdominal disease. Sea-sickness, moreover, is a cerebral affection, thrown on the stomach. So is the sickness produced in many persons by whirling the body, and riding in a carriage with the back toward the horses. The Emperor Napoleon died of a gastric affection, in St Helena, where such complaints are scarcely known. He was, moreover, a very temperate eater; but he had deep sensibility and powerful passions. The most probable cause of his disease, therefore, was mortification at the loss of empire, resentment and chagrin at his exile and confinement, vexation at the treatment he received from the governor of the island, and inconsolable grief at being separated from his family. These causes, goading his brain almost to madness, threw their influence sympathetically on his stomach, and destroyed him.

Nor is the whole yet told. Grief is nothing but a painful and deleterious cerebral irritation. Females experience that passion in its greatest intensity, and it is to them a very productive cause of dyspepsia. So is jealousy, a passion which they also feel with peculiar acuteness and distress. And every painful passion and emotion is but another name for excessive and hurtful irritation of the brain, which, if long continued, never fails to injure digestion. Even anger arrests the progress of digestion. Nor are females the only sufferers from such irritation. Males also are its victims.*

* In 1822, and during several of the following years, a rare opportunity was enjoyed by Dr William Beaumont, an American physician,

A man in perfect health, and with a fine appetite, seats himself at table; but before he has begun his meal, a messenger communicates to him some distressing news. His appetite vanishes, and the very sight and odour of the food become offensive to him. Or, has he just finished his repast, when the message is delivered? If he be not actually sickened by it, and forced to discharge the contents of his stomach, indigestion, sick headach, and perhaps feverishness, are the result. And what student does not know that effects, somewhat similar, are produced by severe intellectual toil immediately after a plentiful meal? That dyspepsia, moreover, is proverbially one of the *morbi studiosorum*, one of the complaints of the studious, is a truth familiar to every one. Nor is it less notorious, that men who think but little, and are exempt from care, seldom suffer from it. The cheerful and jolly do not often become dyspeptic—the grave and care-worn very frequently. This truth has been long and familiarly known. Cæsar manifested his acquaintance with it, when he spoke of the countenances of the gay and cheerful Anthony, and the deeply thoughtful Brutus and Cassius; the former fresh, full, and ruddy, the latter pale, sallow, and care-worn.

of making observations on the physiology of digestion, in the case of a Canadian named Alexis St Martin, into whose stomach an opening was made by the accidental discharge of a musket. The wound healed completely, but the aperture remained, being closed up only by a valve opening inwards. Dr Beaumont availed himself largely of the means of investigation thus happily thrown in his way, and has published the results of his labours in a volume entitled *Experiments and Observations on the Gastric Juice and the Physiology of Digestion. By William Beaumont, M. D., Surgeon in the U. S. Army.* Plattsburgh, 1833. Among other things he remarked, that when the brain was disturbed or depressed by fear, anger, or other disagreeable emotion, the surface of the stomach became sometimes red and dry, and at other times pale and moist, losing altogether its smooth and healthy appearance; and that, when food was swallowed in such circumstances, the usual secretion of the gastric juice necessary for digestion failed to appear. A very full account of this remarkable case will be found in *The Physiology of Digestion, considered with Relation to the Principles of Dietetics. By Andrew Combe, M. D.* Edinburgh, 1836.—R. C.

But my argument is not yet closed. The most successful mode of treating dyspepsia favours the belief that it often arises from cerebral irritation, and is always perhaps connected with it. Am I asked, in what this treatment consists? I reply, in regulating the passions, taking muscular exercise in the open air, abandoning intellectual toil, and retreating for a time from business and care. Unless the complaint be so inveterate and deep-rooted as to have produced some serious organic lesion, this course of treatment, steadily pursued, will cure it, without either the use of much medicine, or confinement to a very strict diet; and it can often be cured in no other way. To him whose brain is constantly on the rack, dyspeptic medicine and diet are of little use.

How often do we find the efficacy of this mode of treatment verified! An individual deeply devoted to books and study becomes dyspeptic. Without mitigating his intellectual labours he tries various remedies for the restoration of his health. For months, and perhaps years, he eats by weight of prescribed articles, and dresses and exercises by measurement and rule. During this trial of his patience, tea and coffee are rejected; new milk, boiled rice, and bread, stale or made of unbolted flour, with fresh eggs and well-prepared mutton chops, being his only food, and water his only drink; and he walks every day, at stated hours, a given number of miles. Finding this treatment ineffectual, he resorts to daily horse-exercise, under an assurance from some very 'skilful doctor,' or perhaps a 'knowing nurse,' that that will cure him; but, instead of being removed, or even lightened, his complaint grows worse. During these experiments, he has continued to return regularly from his meals, and his horse and foot exercise, to his books and his pen, thus irritating and exhausting his brain by uninterrupted labour. At length, impatient of trials that have proved so unavailing, he renounces medicine and regimen, resolves to become master of himself and his movements, and takes his case into his own hands. Under this determination he shuts up his study, mounts his horse, and sets out on a journey, to visit a friend a couple of hundred miles distant, riding during wet weather as well as dry, and living on the common fare of travellers. Before he has proceeded a hundred miles, his health is much improved; and, on reaching the dwelling of his friend, he finds himself well.

This is no fancy case, but one that has innumerable examples in life. To what is the cure to be attributed? The dyspeptic has previously conformed most strictly to dietetic rules, and travelled, on foot and on horseback, some thousands of miles, in fine weather and through a pure atmosphere, without any benefit to health; yet he is now cured by riding two hundred miles, a part of the way in bad weather, and living in the mean time on indifferent food. The cause of the salutary effect of his journey is easily rendered. Having relinquished his intellectual toils, his brain is at ease, and no longer injures his digestive organs or any other part of his system. On the contrary, by acting salutarily on them, it benefits them, and enables them to perform their respective functions. Let him immediately return to his studies with his usual intensity, and his complaint will revisit him. Instead of a man of letters, suppose the dyspeptic to be a statesman, an artist, or a man of business, the result of the specified measures will be the same. Cerebral quietude will contribute much to the restoration of his health.

Again. It is well known that individuals, who, under all sorts of treatment, have been tormented by dyspepsia from the age of twenty-five or thirty to forty or forty-five, very often recover their health, and from having been thin, become fleshy, about the latter period, after having abandoned medicine entirely, and relaxed not a little in the strictness of their regimen. To use their own language, they seem to have ' gotten well without any cause.' A satisfactory cause, however, is not wanting. They are less harassed and corroded by care, passion, and mental labour—in simpler and more philosophical language, they experience less cerebral irritation, for one of the two following reasons, or both united. They have attained the object for which they had previously toiled and disquieted themselves; or age and experience have somewhat blunted their sensibilities, and calmed their passions; or both causes have co-operated to the same end. For similar reasons, dyspepsia rarely commences in an individual after his forty-fifth or fiftieth year. Time has diminished the susceptibility of his brain.

Such appear to be the leading causes of the alarming frequency and increase of madness and dyspepsia in the United States. The same irritation which, in some cases, produces the former complaint, in others gives rise to the latter, by not only disqualifying the brain for acting beneficially on the stomach and the other digestive organs, but by rendering its influence injurious to them. Nor can it be doubted, as already intimated, that Infant Schools, under their present administration, are calculated to increase the evil, by giving a morbid growth and susceptibility to the brain; so, as heretofore mentioned, are intemperate eating, and other improprieties in diet and drink. The only effectual remedy is a well-directed physical education.

Were I asked, how severe cerebral irritation and labour injure the stomach and other digestive organs, my reply would be, In a two-fold way, sympathetically and functionally. In the latter mode, the brain, being unfitted for its healthy action, and in some degree exhausted itself, withholds from the whole digestive system that measure of influence and aid, known to be essential to the performance of its functions. In what this influence consists, is not exactly known. It is probably, however, the product of a subtle and peculiar form of matter, which the brain prepares from the blood, and transmits by the nerves to the other parts of the body. That a communication between the stomach and the brain is necessary to digestion, experiment proves. When that formed by the nerves is interrupted, the digestive action is suspended; when restored, the process again goes on. Since, therefore, the entire want of the cerebral influence injures the stomach, any irregularities or bad qualities in it can scarcely fail to do the same.

Did time permit, it would be gratifying to me to revert to the consideration of the moral influence of the brain, and to speak of it more fully, and in a manner more worthy of its importance, than I have heretofore done. That a sound, well-developed, and well-regulated condition of that organ is as truly the source of correct morals, as a healthy condition of the heart and the lungs is of the due circulation and arterialization of the blood, is a truth admitted now by all who have thoroughly studied the subject, and which is destined, at no very distant period, to be without an opponent. On this ground alone can moral education and reform be rationally and successfully conducted, and brought to the perfection of which they are susceptible. The moral organs of the brain, and the reflecting ones, as their adjuvants, must be strengthened by regular and well-directed exercise, and thus rendered more ready in action, as well as more vigorous. Immorality and crime are the product of the animal organs; and the reason of their being committed is obvious. These organs preponderate, if not habitually, at least for the time, over the moral and reflecting organs. Instead of being subordinate, as they ought to be, they take the mastery, and, by running into excess, bring guilt on the individual; precisely as the crew of a vessel sometimes mutiny, break from the control of their officers, and perhaps murder them and plunder the ship. The source of every crime is the same, the preponderance of the animal portion of the brain; and the radical extinguishment must be also the same—the reduction of the strength of that portion, and its being brought to a state of subordination to the higher organs. Every habitual offender has a brain in some way unsound. There is a want of balance and harmony between his cerebral organs, which amounts to derangement, and calls for skilful treatment to remove it. And, without such treatment, his moral malady will as necessarily continue, as must a dislocated joint remain in a deranged condition if it be not reduced

To carry out the figure; except in far-gone cases, the moral disease can be remedied by judicious treatment, as certainly as the articular. The remedy, moveover, is simple. It consists in bringing the offending animal organs to a state of comparative *inaction*, which will diminish their strength; and give constant exercise to the moral and reflecting organs, by which their power and promptitude in acting will be increased. Thus will the truly *human* portion of the brain attain an ascendency over the *animal*, and man will advance towards the perfection of his nature.

Is any one inclined to request me to be more explicit in pointing out the means of moral education and reform, and in specifying the mode in which the process is to be conducted? If so, I could not answer him better than by directing his attention to several of the penitentiary establishments, and all the houses of correction for juvenile offenders, in the United States. There, to a certain extent, the means are already in operation, and in some of the institutions the prospects are very flattering. In many cases, vicious and criminal propensities have been extinguished, and habits of morality and virtue established. In other words, the inordinate action of the animal organs has been allayed, and that of the moral and reflecting invigorated.

The means of effecting this are few and simple. By being withdrawn from the community, and, in many cases, by solitary confinement, the culprits are strictly guarded not only from the commission of crime, but from all temptation to it. Thus are their animal organs, which are prone to offend, reduced to a state of comparative inaction, which, in time, deprives them of much of their strength, and weakens, in a corresponding degree, the appetite for vice. For the propensity to transgress is but the craving of a powerful and highly excited organ. But this alone could not be denominated moral reform. At most, it would be but negatively so. To weaken one class of organs is not exactly tantamount to the strengthening of another, even though they be antagonists. Other measures therefore are added. The offenders are strictly practised in some form of useful industry, which not only occupies the mind, and withdraws it from thoughts of vice, but is itself a moral duty. Nor is this all. Moral and religious instruction is directly inculcated on them by reading, preaching, conversation, remonstrance, advice, example, and practice. This, by exciting and exercising their moral and reflecting organs, confers on them positive strength, and, except in the worst class of cases, gives them ultimately an ascendency over the animal. Then is the paramount bias of the mind turned towards virtue, and the reformation of the offenders is complete.

When established on correct principles, and skilfully administered, penitentiaries and houses of correction are *moral hospitals*, where criminal propensities are treated as diseases, consisting in unsound conditions of the brain. And in such conditions they do consist, as certainly as hepatitis does in a morbid state of the liver, or dyspepsia in a similar state of the stomach. And by judicious treatment they can be as certainly removed. Nor is it possible on any other principles to purify and strengthen our moral nature, and raise it to the height and confer on it the dignity of which it is susceptible. Yet all this amounts to nothing more than the application of physical education to the moral organs of the brain. In treating of it, therefore, I have not in any degree departed from my subject. I have only brought to bear on it matter of illustration not usually employed, but not on that account the less appropriate and useful. Let me add, that the time and treatment necessary for the removal of a malady must be apportioned and accommodated to its strength, fixity, and aggravating circumstances. And as there are cases of incurable derangement in other parts of the body, so are there in the brain, of that which creates a propensity to crime. In such instances, the interests of society can be duly protected, only by the confinement of the culprits for life, or their capital punishment.

The object of prison-discipline being to strengthen the

higher and better qualities of the criminal, and to weaken those which are leading him astray, let every appliance having the opposite tendency be avoided. Hence ought we to abandon every modification of harsh conduct towards him. By the discipline of blows no moral or intellectual faculty is cultivated. It neither communicates knowledge nor ministers to virtue. It excites smothered resentment, hatred, and fear, awakens and nourishes a propensity to revenge, and teaches caution, concealment, and artifice; and there its influence ends. But these feelings being purely *animal*, and the very reverse of all that is praiseworthy, or that ministers to amendment, its direct and necessary tendency is still more deeply and hopelessly to *brutalize* man, not to reform him. It compels the culprit to regard civil society, by whose authority it is inflicted, as his avowed and inexorable enemy, and, as an inevitable consequence, renders him the self-sworn enemy of the human race. It degrades him, moreover, in his own opinion; and, as already intimated, out of degradation nothing valuable can possibly arise. As well may you attempt, by the infliction of stripes, to excite in the sufferer pleasurable feelings, as either a virtuous emotion or a praiseworthy resolution. Or if, under the smarting of the lash, such a seeming resolution be formed, it is as unstable as passion, and as faithless as hypocrisy. It deceives even him who forms it. Its violation, therefore, is as certain and speedy, as the occurrence of temptation united to opportunity. It is but a house erected on the sand, which the first billow of passion will demolish. It, for a short period, deters from crime, but awakens no disrelish for it.

A system of discipline like this, established for the professed purpose of either meting out impartial justice to criminals and convicts, or producing in them such a reform as to prepare them for the duties of orderly and valuable citizens, is unqualified mockery. Human ingenuity could scarcely devise a scheme more entirely calculated to debase man, confirm him in vice, and unfit him for society, if he were not already unfitted. It savours as little of wisdom and sound policy, as of benevolence and clemency. It is utterly wanting in them all.

Were the convicts sentenced to confinement during life, like the galley-slaves of Barbary, or those who formerly groaned beneath their chains in the mines of Spanish America, and were the object in view merely to preserve order, and enforce labour, within the walls of the penitentiary, such a plan of discipline would be well enough suited to such an end. But, where reform is intended, and the criminals, after a term of years, are to be let loose again on society, the system is calculated to infuriate them against man, to bind them more durably to each other by consociated suffering and mutual sympathy, and train and harden them in their propensities to crime.

Such are the inferences we are compelled to draw from the well-known principles of human nature; and observation and experience confirm their truth. The histories of penitentiaries and their inhabitants teach us, that offenders, dismissed from those places of chastisement, after severe treatment, which they considered tyrannical and unjust, have been too *frequently*, not to use a stronger term and say *always*, more confirmed in their vicious propensities, and more inflexible in their course of malefactions. They have returned, with increased voracity, to their acts of felony, like famished wolves to their ravenous meal. The discipline they have undergone has taught them deeper artifice and more dexterous cunning, and rendered them doubly dangerous to society. But it has never reformed them, and it never can, until causes cease to be followed by their *natural* effects, and produce the *contrary*. If reformation has been effected in them at all, it has been by other means.[*]

In the training of the brain, the proper management

---

[*] Dr Caldwell's opinions regarding the treatment of criminals, are fully expounded in his " New Views of Penitentiary Discipline, and Moral Education and Reformation of Criminals," published in the *Phrenological Journal*, vii. 385, 493.—R. C.

of *sleep* is of considerable moment. Children require more sleep than adults, and some children more than others. Young infants should be allowed to sleep a greater portion of their time. As they advance in years, a less proportion will be not only sufficient, but more salutary to them. For children and youth pursuing their education, from seven to nine hours of sleep out of twenty-four is enough. Many do not require more than six. Less than that might prove injurious, especially if the abstinence were long continued. Too little sleep weakens the brain, and consequently the entire system, by *exhaustion;* too much by *inaction.* For sleep consists in the quietude of the brain. Of this, as of other things, a mean quantity is best. An excess of sleep has produced idiotism; a deprivation of it, madness—and sometimes inflammation of the brain.*

* A late French writer, M. Friedlander, gives the following Table, shewing the hours of sleep, exercise, occupation, and repose, which he conceives to be requisite at different ages in youth:—

Age.	Hours of Sleep.	Hours of Exercise.	Hours of Occupation.	Hours of Repose.
7	9 to 10	10	1	4
8	9	9	2	4
9	9	8	3	4
10	8 to 9	8	4	4
11	8	7	5	4
12	8	6	6	4
13	8	5	7	4
14	7	5	8	4
15	7	4	9	4

I agree with Mr Macnish in thinking that the quantity of sleep here allowed is rather too little for the generality of children. "If an hour were added to it," says he, "it would approximate nearer to the truth. A child of seven or eight, with a very active brain and a tendency to precocity, should be allowed more sleep—perhaps one or two hours more—than a dull child. Seven hours' sleep is certainly too little for growing lads of fourteen. A sufficiency of sleep is as necessary for forming a healthy brain, while that viscus is in the process of growth,

It is not unimportant to observe, that a life of strict temperance curtails materially the time necessary to be spent in sleep. For this there are sundry reasons, two of them leading ones. The intemperate require a greater amount of actual sleep on account of the deeper exhaustion of their systems. But their sleep, never healthy, is broken, dreamy, and comparatively unrefreshing. It is the sleep of bad digestion, their stomachs being oppressed by a superabundance of food. Hence they are compelled to consume a greater length of time in acquiring the necessary degree of repose. The temperate and regular, on the contrary, are comparatively strangers to dreams. They rest profoundly, and enjoy a fuller measure of sound and refreshing sleep in six hours, than the intemperate do in nine. In this way they save, in the course of a lifetime, several years of active and useful existence, which, to those of contrary habits, are lost in sleep and drowsiness.

As neither their bones nor muscles are yet confirmed in strength, the manner in which children hold themselves in school is not unimportant. They should sit as erect as their employments will admit, lest they contract

as a sufficiency of food. At the same time, we must be cautious not to indulge young people in too much sleep; for in this case the brain becomes torpid, as in the other case morbidly irritable. A great deal depends on constitution; the portion of sleep which suffices for one person may not be enough for another. Parents often err greatly in this respect. Finding a certain quantum sufficient for themselves, they conclude that a similar allowance will suffice for their children. The consequence is, that the latter have their constitutions often ruined, and even their intellects impaired. Delicate people of all descriptions, and children in particular, should be allowed a great deal more sleep than the healthy and robust."—(*Remarks on the Influence of Mental Cultivation and Excitement upon Health. By Amariah Brigham, M. D. With Notes by Robert Macnish.* Glasgow, 1836. Note 51.) Dr Brigham, the author of the little work here named, is an enlightened American physician, and has pointed out in a very forcible manner the fruitlessness and absurdity of overworking the brains of children, and likewise the bad effects of studying too much in adult life. Mr Macnish has enhanced not a little the value of the book by the addition of numerous notes.—R. C.

ungraceful and pernicious habits of stooping or distortion; and they ought not to be permitted, much less compelled, to sit long in one position, but be directed to change it, by standing, or in some other way. This will prevent numbness of their limbs, and other unpleasant effects from stillness and compression. Want of motion produces in many a coldness of the feet, which weakens their attention to study, and brings on headach and dyspepsia. In a special manner, children should not be allowed to lean heavily on the breast or stomach, against desks or tables. Gastric derangement and pulmonary consumption have been the issue of such practices. Pupils have often suffered, in their eyes, from a strong glare of light through a window in front of them. Such accidents should be carefully guarded against.

The practice of self-pollution among youth at school, especially in boarding-schools, is much more frequent than is generally imagined. And no vice is more detestable or ruinous. Health, intellect, morals—all purity, dignity, and self-respect sink beneath it, in promiscuous and hopeless ruin. When carried to excess, it produces idiotism in the most deplorable and disgusting form, accompanied by impaired vision and hearing, paralysis, and other distressing infirmities,—and terminates in death. No vigilance to prevent it, therefore, can be too strict; and, when it is detected, no remonstrance against it can be too solemn, no representation of its direful effects too strong, no denunciation of it too stern, and, if persevered in, no penalty for it too heavy. But it inflicts its own penalty, in the entire desolation of the being who perpetrates it. Not confined in its effects to the offenders, it falls as a lasting blight on their posterity. In boarding-schools, moreover, the practice is contagious, spreading from one to another, until many, if not the whole, are polluted. The first culprit detected, therefore, should be removed from the institution, as a moral lazar, dangerous alike to purity and soundness of mind and body. But he ought not to be hopelessly abandoned to his fate. Every practicable expedient to reform him should be adopted and persevered in; and the best plan of reform consists in some active and interesting employment, engaged in with alacrity and industriously pursued —so industriously as to banish idleness, and allow but little time even for amusement; for leisure and idleness are often the source and always one of the nurses of the evil to be corrected. And if all other means fail, marriage should be resorted to, as soon as the individual has arrived at maturity, and is in a condition to form that alliance. This vice occurs in families, as well as in schools. Every where, therefore, in the physical education of youth, its prevention is a point of infinite moment. I shall only add, that, in proportion as the temperament is active, the development of Amativeness full, the moral and reflecting developments deficient, and the individual diffident and easily abashed, is the danger of his contracting the vice. In the same proportion, therefore, should be the exertions made to protect him from it.*

* Respecting this and kindred subjects, children are usually left completely in the dark, so that the most lamentable evils are fallen into without the slightest suspicion on the part of the victims that they are doing wrong. The following remarks of Dr Spurzheim deserve an attentive consideration from all to whose care young persons are entrusted. "Many parents," says he, "are cautious and fearful of speaking of such notions to their children, and do not think of the anxiety with which children look for information of that kind, and of the benefit they may derive from it. Such information, when given by the parents, will be received with confidence and respect. Some young persons will possess reflection enough to attend to their bodily health, from the consideration that their constitution will be communicated to their offspring. I know, positively, that such a proceeding has been more effectual and beneficial than endeavouring to prevent children from acquiring any knowledge of that kind, or to conceal the effects of the disorderly satisfaction of physical love. This propensity deserves the same attention which we pay to hunger and thirst. Both are active without our will; and their activity must be directed. Why should we not have recourse to the understanding as far as possible, to regulate the actions, and employ natural means of correction against natural faults? How can we expect that children should suppress a strong internal feeling, without being acquainted with the bad consequences of its abuses, and with its destination?"—(*View of the Elementary Principles of Education, founded on the Study of the Nature of Man.* 2d edition. London, 1828, p. 58.)—R. C.

Of *dress*, as a means in physical education, I have already spoken. A few further remarks on it, and I shall close my discourse. No article of dress should so compress any portion of the body as to injure the skin, diminish the size and vigour of a muscle, restrict the flexibility of a joint, oppose a hindrance to the innervation of the part, or prevent the free circulation of the blood. If any thing be benefited by unlimited freedom of action, it is the system of man, in its organized capacity—I mean the whole system.

Pinching shoes and boots do much mischief. That they produce tormenting and crippling corns, every body knows in theory, and too many by woful experience. But this is not all, nor even the worst. They check the circulation of the pedal blood, make the feet cold and sometimes aid in chilblaining them, diminish the size of the muscles of the part, and take from their strength, and impede their action, by compressing them. Hence no one too tightly shod either walks with elasticity and grace, or receives from the exercise half the benefit it would otherwise bestow. In truth, he is often injured by it. That an individual may move lightly or firmly, with grace or usefulness, his feet must be springy and free.—But cramping and torturing them by pressure does further mischief. It produces, sympathetically, dyspepsia and headach, and sometimes troublesome affections of the breast. Hæmorrhagy from the nostrils and lungs, and even apoplexy and pulmonary consumption, are occasionally excited by it. I shall only add, that tight shoes disfigure the foot. The ancients were strangers to such torturing articles. Their sandals were light and easy. Hence the free and elegant form of their feet. This is seen in the Venus de Medici, the Perseus, the Antinous, the Apollo Belvidere, and many other choice relics of antiquity. Let the feet of those statues be compared with the feet of *elegantes* and *dandies* of the present day, and the beauty of the former will be found to be transcendent.

The time was, but has fortunately gone by for the present, when buckskin inexpressibles, far tighter than the skins of those whom they tormented, were nearly as bad in the effects they produced. Though not equally painful, they were, in some respects, even more annoying and discomfortable. The first "trying on" of those articles, in which the strength and skill of the maker of them, backed by one or two able-bodied assistants, were indispensable, was a fearful job, especially if the weather had sudorific qualities in it. And when, by a horse-power or two, the garment was at length dragged home, buttoned over the knees, and strapped round the legs, then began the tug for motion. The victim of fashion walked as if some of his joints were anchylosed, and others tightly bandaged on account of recent dislocation. From the waist downward, there was less pliability in him than in the limbs of a centenarian, or a gourmand stiffened by chronic gout. Nor was this all. His blood, being denied a free passage in a downward direction, like that of the Plantagenets "mounted" upwards, made his neck and face swell and his eyes protrude, and turned his cheeks as red as the gills of a fish. This inquisition-work, long persisted in, could not fail to be productive of mischief. The whole, however, being an act of homage at the shrine of fashion, the dandy submitted to it with the devotion of a new-made saint, and the imperturbable firmness of a martyr; and, to test to the uttermost his truth and constancy, getting out of his trammels was sometimes a more awful trial than getting into them.

Most earthly things, like the earth herself on her axis, whirl in a circle. Though cramping inexpressibles, therefore, are with our antipodes now, they will no doubt come back again. It is therefore that I have thought it right to enter my protest against them. They are a sad contrivance in physical education.

Tight cravats, by preventing a full flow of blood to the brain through the arteries, and retarding its return by the veins, do mischief. They operate prejudicially in several ways. That they compress the muscles of the neck, and diminish their size, cannot be doubted. Hence, the necks of the moderns, who wear them, are smaller and less comely than those of the ancients, to whom they were unknown. The manly and elegant form and dimensions, as well as the fine attitude and bearing, of the necks of ancient statues, are themes of universal admiration and praise. And they are, no doubt, chiefly if not exclusively, attributable to the free and uncompressed condition of the necks of their originals. It is observed by travellers, that the peasantry of Lombardy have finer necks than any other peasantry in Europe; and they wear nothing round them.

The diminution of the size of the neck, however, is neither the only nor the greatest evil which tight cravats produce. If, in any case, they restrict the nourishment and vitalization of the brain, by withholding from it a competent supply of arterial, and too long retaining in it an accumulation of venous blood, they necessarily weaken the operations of the mind. This is as certain, as that the reduction of the natural flux of blood to a muscle lessens its vigour. As heretofore stated, the vitality of the brain is derived from the arterial blood; and, other things being equal, as is its vitality so is its perfection as the organ of the mind. Were it possible, without doing an injury to other parts, to augment the constant afflux of healthy arterial blood to the brain, the mental operations would be invigorated by it. I state this opinion confidently, because we often witness its verification. When a public speaker is flushed and heated in debate, his mind works more freely and powerfully than at any other time. Why? Because his brain is in better tune. What has thus suddenly improved its condition? An increased current of blood into it, produced by the excitement of its own increased action. That the blood does, on such occasions, flow more copiously into the brain, no one can doubt, who is at all acquainted with the cerebral sensations which the orator himself experiences at the time, or who witnesses the unusual fulness and flush of his countenance, the dewiness, flashing, and protrusion of his eye, and the throbbing of his carotid and temporal arteries. It is well known, that, while intensely engaged in a memorable debate, last winter, in Washington, a distinguished senator became so giddy, by the inordinate rushing of blood into the brain, that he was obliged to sit down; and the senate adjourned, to give him time to recover. And, more recently, a new member of the House of Representatives fell while speaking, and suddenly expired from the same cause. A member of the law class of Transylvania, moreover, experienced, a few weeks ago, a convulsive affection from a congestion of blood in the head, induced by excessive excitement of the brain in the ardour of debate. Nor is this all. In several individuals, whose brain had been denuded and brought into view by accident or disease, the movement and swelling of the organ were rendered palpable, by the flux of blood into it during intense feeling and active thought. A remarkable case of this description occurred in Montpelier in 1822; and others, somewhat similar, are mentioned by Sir Astley Cooper in his Lectures on Surgery.* Had I leisure, and were it requisite, I could cite numerous instances of a like description. Sudden and deep emotion, as well as the vigorous working of the intellectual powers, has produced phrenitis, palsy, and apoplexy, by a superabundant rushing of blood into the brain. Inordinate excitement, of whatever kind it may be, draws an unusual amount of blood into that organ; and such an amount is essential to the maintenance of the excitement thus brought on.

Believing that a cravat had a bad effect on the operations of his mind, Lord Byron never wore one. Report indeed says, that his reason for this was his desire to shew his neck uncovered, on account of its uncommon beauty. This, however, is probably but a petty slander. His motives were best known to himself. Nor can any one doubt, that immoderate compression of the neck

---

* These cases are more fully noticed by Dr Andrew Combe in his *Principles of Physiology applied to the Preservation of Health, and to the Improvement of Physical and Mental Education.* 4th edition, p. 303.

does mischief. Headach, impaired vision, and hemorrhagy from the nose are among its effects. So, we are told, is apoplexy.

An article of dress remains to be noticed, which is immeasurably worse in its effects than all those whose influence I have considered. Motives of prudence, if not of gallantry, might impose silence on me respecting it, did not a regard for truth and duty, and a wish to be useful, invoke me to speak out. The article makes a part of the *apparel*, I may not say the *ornament* of woman, whose delicacy I would in no case willingly offend, and whose displeasure I would never intentionally incur, except in an effort to do her good. It is probably already conjectured, that my allusion is to corsets. If so, the conjecture is correct. I do allude to corsets, and pronounce them, most seriously, an alarming evil. The crippling machinery, with which the females of China compress and disfigure their feet and ancles, making the former too small, and the latter too thick and clumsy, are innocent to them. Corsets compress and disfigure a portion of the system infinitely more important than the mere termination of the lower extremities. While the Pagan ladies confine their attack to the out-posts of life, the fair Christians assault the citadel. By curtailing the dimensions of two of the great cavities of the body, corsets obstruct the growth and impair the functions of the organs they contain. And it has been already stated, that these are among the governing organs of the body, whose injury or unsound condition proves prejudicial to every other portion of it. I allude to the stomach, liver, and all the other chyle-making and chyle-carrying viscera, and to the heart, lungs, and large bloodvessels. These are all compressed and deranged in their functions, and most of them reduced in their size, removed from their places, and altered in their shape, by tight corsetting. It is in vain to deny the truth of this, as an excuse for disregarding the warning it imparts. The fact can be, and has repeatedly been demonstrated, in anatomical researches. I shall exhibit to you presently satisfactory proof it.

108 PHYSICAL EDUCATION.

To secure to adult females what are called *fine figures*—which mean waists, shoulders, and hips quite out of symmetry with each other, and with the rest of the body—the corset-screws are applied to them while they are young girls, their whole systems being tender, and their bones comparatively soft and flexible. The consequence is, that when the lacing is tight—and it is always *too* tight, for there should be none at all of it—their ribs, especially the false ones, are pressed inwardly to such an extent, that their front ends nearly touch each other, if they do not actually overlap; whereas, in their natural position, they are wide apart.* Even the upper ribs are,

* A view of the bones of the thorax is here subjoined, that the deleterious effects of tight-lacing may be rendered the more apparent. These bones are, 1st, the sternum or breast-bone *a*; 2d, the spine *b b*; and, 3d, the ribs *c c c c*. The anterior extremity of each rib is composed not of bone, but of elastic cartilage. The seven uppermost, which are immediately connected with the sternum, are called the *true ribs*; to the remaining five the appellation *false ribs* is given. It is

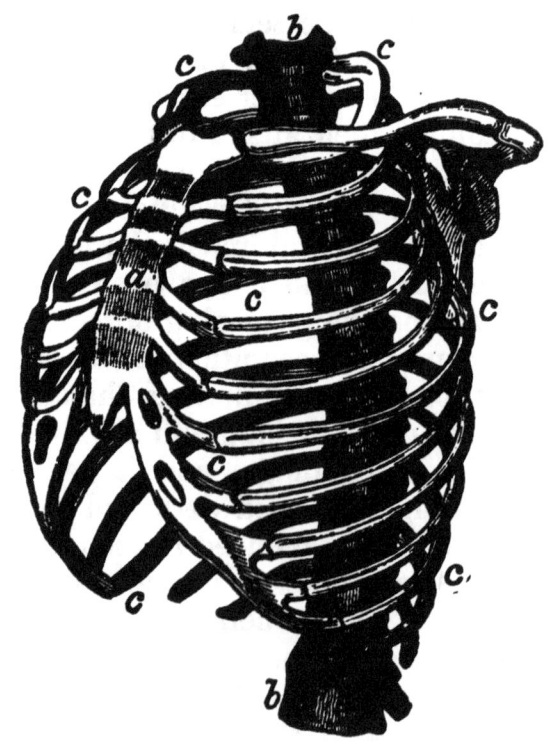

at times, so pressed on, as to be flattened, or rather straightened, in their lateral arches, and protruded forward, carrying along with them the breast-bone, to which they are attached. Thus is the whole trunk of the body *altered* in its figure and dimensions, but not *improved*. Far from it. All is for the worse, as well in appearance as in effect. The abdominal cavity being in this way preternaturally straightened in a horizontal direction, its viscera are pressed inordinately upward against the diaphragm. That membrane being thus forced upward also compresses in its turn the lungs, heart, and large bloodvessels, and brings them more or less into collision with the thoracic duct, obstructing in some degree the movement of the chyle. In this forced and unnatural condition of things, all the functions of these viscera, so fundamentally necessary not merely to the well-being of the system but to its very existence, are deranged by compression. Let us glance, in detail, at the mass of mischief thence arising.

obvious from the cut that the lower part of the chest is much more compressible than the upper. The natural shape of the cavity resembles that of a bee-hive, the greatest width being at the lower extremity ; yet by the use of corsets the false ribs are so much bent inwards, that this arrangement is totally reversed. The impiety of the notion that it is possible to improve, by human devices, the natural shape which God has bestowed on the female person, is alluded to by Downman in his didactic poem *Infancy* :—

> " Heaven ! that the human mind,
> Warped by imagination, should believe,
> Or e'en suggest it possible, the form,
> Whose archetype the Deity himself
> Created in His Image, could be changed
> From its divine proportion, and receive
> From alteration, comeliness and grace !
> That round the zone which awkwardly reduced
> E'en to an insect ligament the waist,
> The blooming loves should sport, enticing charms,
> And young attractions !"

The reader will find instructive expositions of the evils of tight-lacing in the *Phrenological Journal*, vol. vii. p. 577, and the *Penny Magazine*, No. 58, 2d March 1834.—R. C.

The whole digestive apparatus being impaired in its action, dyspeptic affections follow; neither is a sufficient amount of wholesome chyle formed, nor of bile secreted, both of which are so indispensable to a sound state of the blood and in other respects so important to the system; and the sympathetic influence of the unhealthy organs on the other parts of the body is rendered deleterious. Add to this, that the compressed organs themselves, being weakened, are unusually liable to further disease from the action of any morbific cause.

The lungs being enfeebled and deranged, not only is respiration defective, and the blood imperfectly matured and vitalized, but they themselves, in common with the stomach, liver, and other associated parts, are in a state of increased liability to additional suffering. Hence hæmoptysis, pulmonary consumption, and dropsy of the chest, often ensue. I knew a young female of some distinction, as respected both her mind and family, in the city of New York, who, some years ago, became known, from tight corsetting, by the name of the " Lady with the small waist!" Notwithstanding her good sense in other things, this excited her ambition to render herself still more worthy of the title, and to prevent, if possible, in others all competition for it. She therefore increased the tightness of her corsets, until she became hump-shouldered, and died in consumption. Nor did any one doubt that her corsets were the cause. She was married, and left an infant son, who, from the slenderness of his frame, and the delicacy of his constitution, is threatened with his mother's complaint. He inherits her *corset-broken* constitution.

Of the heart, the same is true. From its compressed and debilitated condition, it becomes affected with palpitation, dropsy, inflammation, or some other malady—perhaps aneurism—and is incompetent to the vigorous circulation of the blood. Hence every portion of the system suffers—the brain and nerves not excepted; they depending, like other organs, on the arterial blood for their health and power of action. Even the nerves of the organs subjected to pressure are mechanically injured. Since the introduction of corsets as an article of dress, diseases of the heart, among females, are much more frequent than formerly; and they have been traced to that cause in innumerable instances. Cases of the kind could be easily cited. Respecting scirrhous and cancerous affections of the breasts, in women advanced in life, the same is true. Those complaints are far more prevalent now than they were before the present ruinous style of lacing.

From the foregoing view of their destructive effects on the female system, added to another which motives of delicacy forbid me to mention,* it is neither unjust nor extravagant to say of corsets, that they threaten a degeneracy of the human race. And, were they worn by all

---

* My allusion will be readily understood to be to that diminution of the abdominal cavity, which prevents the full expansion of the gravid uterus. This necessarily diminishes the size and vigour of the fœtus in a corresponding degree, and implants in it the elements of future disease. For unnatural compression can scarcely injure it less before birth than after it. Premature parturition is often the effect of this forced and restricted condition of the organs.

Let me not be told that females lay aside their corsets, or loosen them greatly, during gestation. That matters but little. The damage is already done, and cannot be repaired. The diminution, I mean, of the abdominal cavity is already produced, and rendered *permanent*, by the pressure of the ribs inwardly, and their having become fully ossified, and fixed in that position. So confident were the Spartans of the importance attached to the full dimension of the abdominal cavity of females, that they prescribed by law the form of dress they were to wear during pregnancy; and its leading feature was its *looseness*, that it might produce no injurious pressure. I need scarcely add, that the Spartans surpassed the other inhabitants of Greece, in their size, strength, and hardihood, as well as in their fine personal proportions.

An agriculturist has a stock of beautiful and valuable horses. What effect would he produce on their progeny, by so bandaging the females, when young, as to take from their abdominal cavities a third of their size?—I answer, *deep deterioration*. Nor is that produced on the human family, by a similar practice, less striking. Were the higher classes of the inhabitants of Europe larger and stronger a few centuries ago, than they are now? They were not the descendants of corsetted mothers.

females, as they are by many, they would as certainly produce it, as an impaired fruit-tree yields faded fruit—and on the same ground. *The descendants of tight-corsetted mothers will never become the luminaries and leaders of the world.* The mothers of Alexander and Hannibal, Cæsar and Napoleon, never distorted their persons by such a practice. Nor is the whole mischief of those articles yet summed up.

The straightness of the spinal column depends on the strength of the muscles that support it. But those muscles are enfeebled by the pressure of corsets. Hence the spine bends and becomes distorted. Instances of crooked spine have been fearfully multiplied in the fashionable female circles of Europe and America, since the beginning of the present century; while in Greece, Turkey, Persia, Arabia, and other parts of Asia, as well as in Africa, where no tight forms of dress are thought of, it is almost unknown. Nor does it appear among our own countrywomen whose persons are suffered to retain the shape which God intended for them. This breach of his law, therefore, inflicts the penalty incurred by the fault.

It appears, from actual computation, that, of the females who have been accustomed from early life to tight corsetting, nearly *one-fourth* have some unnatural and disfiguring flexure of the spine! By not a few observers and calculators the proportion is maintained to be much greater. A Scottish gentleman of distinction assures us, that he has examined about *two hundred* young females, in fashionable boarding-schools, and that scarcely one of them was free from some sort of corset-injury. Those whose spines were not distorted, had unsightly effects produced on their shoulder-blades, collar-bones, or some other part of the chest, which stuffing and wadding would be requisite to conceal. Some were hunch-backed, and in not a few one shoulder was higher than the other; effects which, in our own country, are much more frequent than is generally suspected. In no individual case was personal symmetry amended by the practice; while in almost every one it was impaired, and in many destroyed. In fact, such pressure cannot fail to injure the symmetry of the trunk, that being its direct tendency. The custom, therefore, is as foreign from correct taste, as from sound philosophy—and I was near saying, from humanity and moral rectitude.*

Woman was not intended to be turned by artificial means into an insect, with broad square shoulders, and a spindle-waist. The latter portion of her body was designed to be something more than skin and bone. For her benefit as well as for the elegance of her form, Nature has surrounded it with substantial muscles, and cellular tissue, which ought not to be sported with and wasted, in compliance with fashion and a spurious taste. And she may rest assured, that she is not only more healthy, vigorous, and comfortable, but also an object of greater attraction, with a flexible and fleshy, than with a shrivelled, stiffened, and skinny waist. Nor are the female shoulders broad and square by *nature*, which alone gives patterns of real beauty. An attempt to render them so by art, therefore, is equally repugnant to correct taste and sound judgment. Yet such is the effect of tight corsetting. Preventing the blood from circulating freely through the muscles of the lower part of the trunk, or rather of its middle, it throws it into those of its upper portion, preternaturally nourishing and enlarging them, and raising and squaring the shoulders, and rendering them pointed. The mere mechanical action of corsets

---

* Dr Barlow of Bath, who has given, in the *Cyclopædia of Practical Medicine* (Article EDUCATION, PHYSICAL, vol. i. p. 693), an admirable exposition of the baneful effects of tight-lacing—"those horrible ravages in female health," as he justly terms them, " that result from the visceral lesions which the tyranny of fashion occasions"—makes the forcible remark, that " to any one impressed with the reality and extent of the evils here deprecated, it is difficult to think or write on them with perfect calmness." The same enlightened and eminent physician has published a valuable treatise on the spinal curvature thus occasioned, and the means of removing it, in the fifth volume of *The Midland Medical and Surgical Reporter.*—R. C.

contributes to the latter effect, by forcing upward the muscles of the chest, together with the upper ribs, shoulder-blades, and collar-bones. And time renders the deformity permanent. No woman who has worn tight corsets from her girlhood, has, or ever will have, those important parts of her frame in their proper places: they are all more or less dislocated, and the effect produced is a direct deviation from beauty of form. Burke, in speaking of the fascinating elegance of the female bust, in his treatise on the " Sublime and Beautiful," gives a description of it extremely different from the bust of a well-corsetted fashionable of the present day. His just and glowing picture is made up entirely of easy slopes and graceful curve lines. We have too much now of points, angles, and masculine squareness. Yet the female figure, when not put out of shape, is as beautiful now as it was then. Independently of the injury done to health, the personal disfiguration produced by tight corsets, hogshead skirts, and shoulder balloons, is a lasting reproach on the taste of the times.

It is to man that nature has given broad, square, and brawny shoulders, and a waist comparatively narrow; and, so far as tight corsets and other articles of dress may avail, woman is usurping his figure. I need scarcely add, that in grace and beauty of person, which confer on her much of her attractiveness and power, and should therefore be among the cherished objects of her ambition, she is losing greatly by the change. Man submits to woman, and courts her approbation and smiles; his best affections cling to her, and his arm and life protect her, on account of her womanly qualities. Any thing masculine in her excites his *dissatisfaction*, not to give the feeling a stronger name; and broad square shoulders *are* masculine, suited only to a man and a virago. There is in them nothing of that delicacy, appeal for protection, and all-subduing loveliness, which we instinctively attach to the word *feminine*. Instead of doing aught, therefore, to create in herself such a form of person, woman should shun it as she would deformity of any other kind.

I have said that tight corsetting, obstructing the free passage of the blood downward, throws it into the superior portion of the trunk. But it does more; it forces it in preternatural quantities, but impaired in quality, into the head, and produces there many forms of disease that are painful and annoying, and some that are dangerous. Among these are headach, giddiness, bleeding from the nose, imperfect vision and other affections of the eyes, noise in the ears, convulsions, and apoplexy. Fainting is another effect of this preternatural accumulation of blood in the brain, the reason of which is plain. While the corsets are on and laced, a sufficient quantity of blood is sent to the brain, to enable that organ to sustain, by its influence, the heart and muscles of voluntary motion, and hold them to their functions. As soon, however, as the corsets are unlaced, the blood forsakes the brain, in part, and flows naturally through its downward channels. The consequence is obvious. The brain being thus enfeebled, for want of the blood necessary for its vitality and the functions it performs, and its invigorating influence being no longer extended to the system generally, the heart and muscles fail in their action, and the individual faints. This occurrence takes place on the same ground with fainting from venesection, or any other form of hemorrhagy. Too much blood is withdrawn from the brain. That viscus is deprived, of course, of much of its own vitality and power to act. Nor is this all: it is deprived also of much of the material from which prepares its sustaining influence for the body generally; for whatever the matter of cerebral influence may be, it is prepared from the blood as certainly as bile and saliva are.

Almost all females who lace tightly complain of weakness when their corsets are removed, and many of them are obliged to assume a horizontal posture to escape asphyxia. Worse still: some are compelled to wear their corsets as a part of their night-dress! Even a horizontal posture does not secure them from a tendency to faint. This is so deplorable a condition, that the practice which induces it involves criminality. Many acts are called felonious, and made punishable by law, which, contrasted with it, are innocent. By permitting it, parents, especially mothers, assume a responsibility which might well make them tremble. They are accessory to its consequences, however fatal. Indeed, possessing as they do full powers of prevention, they should be considered principals.

Perhaps all females who wear corsets, though they may not faint on removing them, nor even feel a tendency to that effect, complain of uneasiness and debility in the back, or some other part of the trunk. The reason is plain. The muscles of the part being weakened by pressure, require the continuance of it, as the sot does the stimulus of his dram, to give them tone and strength sufficient to sustain the weight of the body in an erect position. Hence the individual bends the trunk ungracefully; and, unless the vigour of the muscles be restored, she is threatened with a spinal curvature.*

Even beauty of countenance is impaired, and in time

---

* Many women of intelligence and experience are inclined to believe, that some form of bracing around the female waist is, if not essential, highly useful, in giving support to the body, and maintaining its erect posture. This is a mistake. Such artificial support is required only as a consequence of disease, or from the debilitated condition of the muscles by previous tight lacing. True—the muscles of the female body are feebler than those of the male; but, corresponding to this, the weight of the body is less. In consequence of this fitness, the trunk of woman requires, by nature, no more artificial aid to keep it straight than the trunk of man. Hence the elegance of the female form in Georgia, Circassia, and other parts of Asia, where tightness of dress is unfashionable and unknown. The necessity of corsets, therefore, to sustain the person, arises from the misfortune of having ever worn them; and, unless the practice be abandoned, that misfortune, like other constitutional defects, will pass from mother to daughter in an increasing ratio, until it shall result in a fearful degeneracy of our race.—[Nor is it only by the pressure of the corsets that the muscles of the back are weakened. Being supplanted in their office of supporters of the trunk, they lose their efficiency through want of exercise. Like the muscles of the limbs, they suffer a diminution of strength if not sufficiently employed.—R. C.]

destroyed, by tight corsets. Do you ask me in what way? I answer, that those instruments of mischief wither in the complexion the freshness of health, and substitute for it the sallowness of disease—on the spot where the rose and the ruby had shed their lustre, they pour bile and sprinkle ashes. They do still more, and worse. They dapple the cheek with unsightly blotches, convert its fine cuticle into a motley scurf, blear the eyes, discolour the teeth and dissolve them by caries, and tip the nose with cranberry red. That effects of this description often result from gastric and hepatic derangement, every practitioner of medicine knows; and it has been already shewn that such derangement is produced by corsets.

But those articles make still more fatal havock of female beauty, by imprinting on the countenance—not premature wrinkles—that could be borne—but marks of the decay of *mental beauty*—I mean deep and indelible lines of peevishness, fretfulness, and ill-temper, the bitter result of impaired health. No form of indisposition so incurably ruins the temper of woman as that which prematurely destroys her beauty, especially if she feels conscious that her own indiscretions have been instrumental in its production. To the truth of this experience testifies. Independently, moreover, of their cause, no other complaints pour into the temper such acerbity and bitterness as those of the digestive organs. This also is the result of experience. Man, but more especially woman, bears fever, pulmonary consumption, fractures, wounds, and other forms of injury and disease, with a patience and mildness, which, if they do not improve her personal beauty, increase her loveliness, and add tenfold to the sympathy and sorrow felt for her suffering. But dyspeptic affections—especially, I repeat, if a busy and tormenting consciousness whispers hourly into her ear that she has herself contributed to their production by a practice she might have avoided, and of the ruinous effects of which she was repeatedly warned—complaints of this description are submitted to by her in a different spirit. She becomes irritable, capricious, gloomy, and full of complaints and fearful imaginings. Unhappy in herself, she seems, in contradiction of her nature, to forget or disregard the happiness of others, and does not even shrink from proving the bane of it. I intend not these remarks as a censure on woman. Far from it. I mean them as a denunciation—and would that it were exterminating—of the abominable practice that destroys her peace and mars her loveliness.

Under this head I shall only add, that, in the higher walks of life, our fair countrywomen, especially in the Southern States, are more delicate and feeble in constitution, and therefore less robust in health, than they are in Europe—more so, certainly, than they are in Great Britain, France, or Germany. The slenderness of their frames, and the semi-pallidness of their complexions, testify to this. It is noticed by all strangers of observation, and cannot be otherwise regarded than as an evil ominous of the degeneracy of our descendants. Women constitutionally feeble cannot be the mothers of a vigorous offspring. There is reason to fear that this fragile delicateness will, by means of a spurious taste, pass into an element of female beauty in the United States, and that will render it a national evil to endure for ages. That this will be the case is not to be doubted, unless the proper remedy be applied. Nor is that remedy unknown, of difficult application, or of dubious effect. It consists in a well-directed physical education. That that will remove the evil, appears from the fact, that the females of our country, in the middle and lower ranks of life, who take sufficient exercise in the open air, and do not injure themselves by their modes of dress, are as healthy and vigorous as any in the world. No man of taste wishes to see our highly cultivated women with milkmaid complexions or harvest-field persons; but had they a little more of both than they now possess, they would be not only more comfortable in themselves, but more lovely in the eyes of others. In the European countries referred to, cultivated females neither house themselves so much, nor marry at so early an age, as they do in the United

States. Hence their health is better, and their frames stronger.

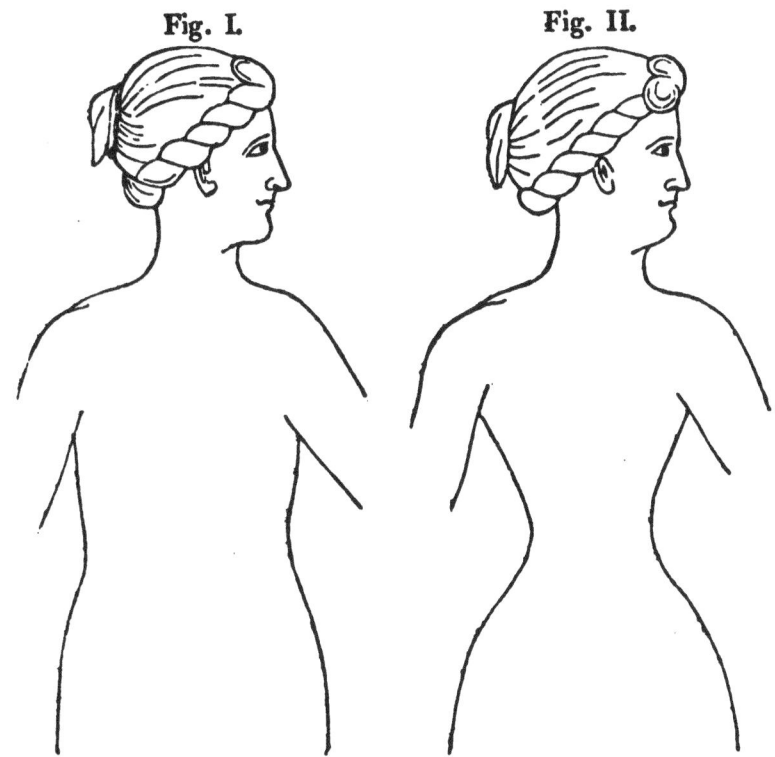

Fig. I.   Fig. II.

Before I close my discourse, allow me to exhibit to you two figures. No. I. is a correct outline of the Venus de Medici, the *beau ideal* of female symmetry, and No. II. that of a well-corsetted modern beauty; and it might be sufficient comment simply to say, ' Look on this picture, and on this.' One has an artificial insect waist, the other the natural waist of woman. One has sloping and graceful shoulders, while the shoulders of the other are comparatively elevated, square, and angular. The proportion of the corsetted female below the waist is also a departure from the symmetry of nature.

Suppose two statues, as large as life, accurately executed, one of them resembling the ancient and the other the modern beauty, which would be preferred, even by the taste of the present day? The question requires no reply. A suitable answer rises spontaneously in the mind of every one. The modern statue would be pronounced ' deformity'—perhaps a ' fright;' the other a miracle of beauty: and the decision would be just.

I know of but *one other* custom, so perfectly calculated to produce a degeneracy of the human race, as that of contracting the dimensions of the waist of woman, weakening her constitution, and distorting her spine; and even *that* is, in some respects, less injurious. I allude to the practice of the Caribs, the most brutal and ferocious tribe of American Indians, in *flattening their heads*. Nor does the custom of the savage produce deformity more real than that of the civilized and fashionable female. Yet the effects of the one are looked on with professed admiration, while those of the other are regarded with horror. Compared to either of them, the practice of the Chinese ladies, as already stated, in disfiguring their feet and ancles, is taste and innocence.

Finally. One of the leading benefits to be bestowed on our race, by Physical Education judiciously practised and carried to the requisite extent, is the production and preservation of a well-adjusted balance, not only between the different portions of the brain, but of the whole body. Few persons, if any at all, bring into life with them a system perfectly balanced in all its parts. Some organs predominate in size and strength, while others are comparatively small and feeble. This is a tendency to disease, and can be removed or amended only by competent training. Let it never be forgotten that the proper exercise of a part, and *that alone*, increases both its bulk and power, and at the same time diminishes any excess of sensitiveness it may possess; and this is precisely what small and feeble parts require, to place them on a par with others, and secure their health. To illustrate my meaning, and show it to be true:—

Is the chest of a boy narrow, and are his lungs weak and irritable? Let those parts be habitually exercised, according to the directions already given, and such a change may be produced in him as will give an equipoise to his body and prevent disease. His chest and lungs may be enlarged not a little, and as well secured from complaints as his other organs. From the free and constant exercise which their calling gives to their arms, shoulders, and thoracic walls and viscera, London boatmen have large chests, and are strangers to consumption. The loud and habitual call, moreover, by which they announce their business and solicit employment, aids in the development and strengthening of their lungs. From these causes, though perpetually exposed to the damp and chilling air of the Thames, they rarely experience any form of pectoral disease.

Of every small and feeble part of the system the same is true. A judicious scheme of training will enlarge and strengthen it. But hereditary predisposition to disease is nothing else than the want of an equipoise between all the different portions of the body. Some organs being comparatively weak and sensitive, are preternaturally prone to actual derangement. By well-directed exercise, therefore, continued through successive generations, may every predisposition of the kind be eradicated.

Such are my views, briefly and imperfectly, but, I trust, intelligibly sketched, of physical education, and the true mode of permanently improving the condition of man. The scheme has in it nothing that is either abstract, visionary, or obscure. Or if it has, I am unable, by the strictest scrutiny, to detect it. It is founded, if I mistake not, on well-known laws of the human constitution. Nor is it in any degree impracticable. It requires but resolution, perseverance, and self-control, connected with intelligence in the use of means that are accessible, and the work is done. Its essence consists in this: let man be so reared that his health may be sound, and so cultivated that his higher powers may have due supremacy over his lower; in other words, that he may be less of an animal, and more of a human being; and his standing will then be as high, and his condition as happy, as his situation and the laws of his being admit.

That my views on these subjects will be all and immediately received as correct, I am neither so vain nor so sanguine as to imagine. Perhaps they do not merit such a reception. But be that as it may, there is one reason why some persons will admit them with great caution, and others probably reject them unexamined. They are tinctured with phrenology, a science which the uninformed and illiberal have proscribed. However deep may be the regret which this excites in me, it neither mortifies nor discourages me. The path I have trodden for years, on this subject, has been carefully explored by me, in its character and bearing: I have reason therefore to believe that I understand it better than those who have never even approached it; and my confidence in its soundness and direction is unlimited. Its course is over safe and solid ground; and it will never allure me, by faithless phantom lights, into dangerous moors or inextricable entanglements. I know phrenology to be true, in its details as well as in its principles, and surpassingly useful in its application and effects. The Book of Nature, which is in the handwriting of the living God, and bears on every page the ineffaceable impress of his glorious signet, amply testifies to its correctness; and, notwithstanding the thousand forms of obstinate and artful opposition it has encountered, the world is already experiencing its benefits. With all who have honestly examined it, its triumph is complete. If there be any labours of my life in which I would presume to glory, they are those which mark me as its steady adherent. And should men, in after times, condescend to remember my name in kindness, their chief reason for the favour will be, that I have dared to be the friend of phrenology, while most of my contemporaries have been its foes—and have never shrunk from raising my voice, or employing my feeble pen, in its defence, through every stage of the long, ungenerous, and embittered persecution it has been made to sustain.

THOUGHTS

ON THE

STUDY OF THE GREEK AND LATIN LANGUAGES.

THE remarks in the present essay, were suggested on reading a pamphlet, entitled, "Reports on the Course of Instruction in Yale College, by a Committee of the Corporation and the Academical Faculty." It is a pamphlet calculated, for sundry reasons, to make no common impression wherever it is read. It is from the pen of scholars, and is written with ability; and, from having been long engaged in the business of "Instruction," most of those concerned in the authorship of it have a fair claim to be deemed qualified judges of the subject of which it treats. Hence, on most points embraced in their "Reports," we consider the sentiments of the Committee correct, their illustrations satisfactory, and their reasons conclusive; and such we presume is the general opinion.

On one point, however, we are *not* satisfied; and it is that on which the Committee appear to have bestowed most attention, and for the decision of which, in conformity to their own views, they were probably most solicitous. We allude to the *necessity* of a knowledge of Greek and Latin, as an *element of a liberal education*. Is it true that that element is *indispensable*; and that no form or degree of education is liberal *without it?* May not an individual, without being versed in the dead languages, be so educated, as to be competent to the highest and most perfect achievements in science, literature, and the arts, as well as in professional life?

These are questions of deep concern to the interests of society, education being the only means of fully developing the human faculties, and conferring on man the entire perfection of which he is susceptible. The Committee have answered the first of them *affirmatively*, and the last, of course, in *the negative*. They have pronounced an acquaintance with Greek and Roman literature *essential* in the constitution of a liberal education.

Before offering any strictures on this decision, we shall simply remark, that we are friendly to the cultivation of ancient literature, under proper restrictions. We disclaim all connexion and sympathy with that class of innovators that would " drive the ploughshare of destruction" through *all* our academies and colleges, and uproot in them every remnant of the learned languages. Though advocates of a temperate and judicious reform on this subject, we deprecate revolution. Indeed, such are the evils inseparable from revolution during its progress, that it should never be attempted in any thing of moment, except as the result of necessity, or under a prospect deemed infallible of great improvement. We shall only add, that we have never witnessed what we considered an unbiassed discussion of the topic before us. Notwithstanding our belief that the learned Committee, whose " Reports" we are about to examine, endeavoured to divest themselves of prepossession and prejudice, and to discover and communicate truth, on the subject of their deliberation, we are compelled to question their ability to do so. In saying this, we intend neither an impeachment of their integrity, nor a disparagement of their understanding. In the former we repose entire confidence, and have already acknowledged the latter to be of a respectable order. We simply mean, that men educated, employed, and habituated from their youth to think, as they have been, must have had, from the well known laws of the human mind, a bias and friendliness of feeling, *apart from their judgment*, in favour of the study of Greek and Latin. To have felt otherwise—we mean, to have felt *impartially*—would have been unnatural, and, perhaps we might add, *unamiable;* a susceptibility of attachment to familiar objects and customary pursuits, being one of the attractive features of the human character. Besides, not to have decided as they did, would have been a censure on themselves and their profession; some of them, we believe, being concerned in teaching the classics, and all of them sanctioning that course of instruction. And self-condemnation, always an unwelcome task, is much increased in its difficulty and repulsiveness, by having to grapple with pride of opinion, personal interest, and confirmed habit.

One more preliminary, and we shall commence our discussion. What are we to understand by a *liberal education?* Unless this question be previously solved, reasoning on the subject can be of no avail. It is fortunate, however, that the committee have given *their* solution of it in the following sentence:—

" By a liberal education, it is believed, has been generally understood, such a course of discipline in the arts and sciences, as is best calculated, at the same time, both to strengthen and enlarge the faculties of the mind, and to familiarize it with the leading principles of the great objects of human investigation and knowledge."

To this solution we offer no other objection than that it is not sufficiently full. The word *all* should have been inserted before " faculties." A liberal education, then, we would define that course of instruction which is best calculated to prepare the mind, by expanding and invigorating *all* its faculties,* for the highest achievements, of which it is capable, in science and letters, as well as in the learned professions and the arts; for, although it is true, as the committee allege, that a liberal is distinct from a professional education, it is equally so that the

---
* All that are not already strong enough, or too strong.—R. C.

latter should always include the former, and is defective without it.

It being conceded, then, that a liberal education consists in a competent cultivation of *all the faculties* of the mind, it must be also conceded, that whatever form of education thus cultivates them *is liberal*. The question may therefore be put, and the Committee have an interest in answering it, What faculty, or what number of faculties, are disciplined and strengthened by the study of Greek and Latin, which cannot be as highly disciplined and strengthened without it? Greek and Latin are but languages. The study of them alone, therefore, is far from invigorating *every* faculty of the mind. When pursued as it usually is, it invigorates only the faculty of language. It in no degree strengthens, or in any way improves, either the reflecting faculties, or the general powers of perception and judgment. It adds nothing to the capacity of the mind to form ideas of number, quantity, weight, figure, size, duration, colour, place, tune, or beauty; nor has it any bearing on comparison, reasoning, wit, or imitation. Yet these are all ideas and operations, conceived and performed by distinct primitive faculties, which education is intended to train and strengthen. We repeat, that the study of language cultivates alone the faculty of language; and that can be cultivated as *certainly*, and we believe as well, by the study—we mean the thorough study—of modern as of ancient languages. This will be made to appear more fully hereafter; but we are running ahead of our inquiry; we are advancing some of our own views, before examining those contained in the pamphlet.

The Committee have assigned their reasons for deciding that the study of the ancient classics is an indispensable constituent of a liberal education. If those reasons are conclusive, the controversy is settled, and any further agitation of it would be worse than nugatory; it would be a waste of time. If, on the contrary, the reasons are invalid, the question is still open, and invites to a stricter examination of the subject of it. Nor ought the invitation to be declined, relating, as it does, to matters of deep and general concern. Our first business, therefore, is to endeavour to test the soundness and sufficiency of some of the positions which the " Reports" maintain.

The Committee first attempt to draw a parallel between the objections made by some persons to the study of mathematics, and those made to the study of Greek and Latin; and, having shewn satisfactorily the invalidity of the former objections, they content themselves with the inference that the latter are equally invalid. In this effort, however, to maintain themselves, they have failed. Arguments founded on analogy should be advanced with caution. They are not philosophical. To illustrate is all they can do. Proof is beyond their sphere. In most instances they do more harm than good, unless they are sustained by something solid and direct to the point. In the present case, moreover, we deem the analogy defective. The attempt to shew that there is an equal necessity for studying the ancient classics and mathematics, we consider a failure. A knowledge of mathematics, if not essential, is highly useful in almost every department of life.* The power of man is greatly augmented by it, and his general efficiency in the same degree improved. It is an important element of practical science, and not only is indispensable in public and weighty projects, but facilitates and renders more complete the transaction of many private and domestic af-

* We do not mean to contend that every candidate for a liberal education ought to be *compelled* to study mathematics to any great extent. Some knowledge of the principles of the science, and their application, he ought to acquire; and to this attainment every one is competent. But those alone who have the faculty of Number in sufficient strength, can attain a thorough knowledge of mathematics. Nor should the attainment be exacted of any others. A practice the contrary of this is unjustifiable, because it leads to an unprofitable consumption of time. Of every other study the same is true. No one should be constrained to pursue it, unless he possesses a faculty for it. A strict observance of this rule would be an important improvement in the education of youth.

fairs. Its influence, like that of the sun and the atmosphere, is felt everywhere, without always being referred to its proper source. Were it necessary to illustrate or prove this, facts suited to either purpose could be collected abundantly from every quarter. Indeed, an extinction of the knowledge of mathematics would not only arrest the progress of improvement, and render useless most improvements already made, but would reduce society to an infantile condition. Every one actively engaged in agriculture, commerce, or the arts, does many things on mathematical principles, whether he be educated in the science or not. Several other sciences, moreover, as well as most of the arts, are dependent on mathematics, if not for their existence, at least for the degrees of perfection they have attained.

As respects a knowlege of Greek and Latin, the case is different. To say the least, its usefulness in the *common affairs* of life, whether public or private, on a large scale or a small one, is very limited. Were we to deny it altogether, it is doubtful whether we could be convicted of error. Classical knowledge belongs to literature, and appears to us to have no necessary connexion with practical science. As a mere attainment in language, it deals in words and names, not in substantial ideas and things. True—it facilitates the making of additions, when required, to scientific nomenclature. Such additions, however, *might* be made without it, though not, perhaps, so conveniently—certainly not so learnedly. But no one will contend that it contributes, in the slightest degree, to widen the boundaries of science, by leading either to further discoveries in the laws of nature, or to new and useful applications of those already made. Some of the most distinguished discoverers, inventors, and improvers, the world has produced, have been strangers to Grecian and Roman literature. In proof of this, many well-known names might be cited.* Of a know-

---

* It would not, we believe, be difficult to show, that of the most illustrious discoverers, inventors, and improvers in science and the arts, a large majority have been ignorant of Greek and Latin. For this

ledge of mathematics, it need scarcely be said that the reverse of this is true. Science and the arts, we repeat, are immeasurably indebted to it, on the score of both discovery and improvement. We reiterate, therefore, our inability to perceive any analogy, at all available in the present case, between the necessity of it, and a knowledge of the ancient classics, constituting an element of a liberal education. Every enlightened people is, and always has been, indebted to mathematics for many of their means of prosperity and power. But nations and empires have been prosperous and powerful, without any aid from Greek or Latin. From reasoning by analogy, the Committee proceed to another ground of argument, which we think no better—that of *authority and fashion.*

"In the British islands (say they), in France, Germany, Italy, and, indeed, in every country of Europe in which literature has acquired distinction and importance, the Greek and Roman classics constitute an *essential* part of a liberal education."

This is begging the question; or rather, assuming positively the right to decide it by the weight of opinion. The allegation made is true only by construction—true on the ground of human authority, but not therefore necessarily so under the sanction of reason. In the coun-

there seems to be a good reason. Self-taught men are untrammelled by authority. They think for themselves, and take nature for their guide; whereas the educated, being much under the influence of what they have learned in colleges and other seats of learning, *think as they have been taught*, and are guided by example. Under these circumstances, the former can scarcely fail to take a lead in the work of general innovation and improvement. The remedy for this evil in our colleges and universities is obvious and easy. Young men should be instructed *reasonably*, not *dogmatically* or *authoritatively*. They should be taught independence of mind, to study nature as well as books, and, on every subject, to examine strictly, believe cautiously, and think for themselves. The following are a few, out of many that might be named, of eminent discoverers, inventors, and improvers, who had no knowledge of Greek and Latin: Franklin, Rittenhouse, Watt, Arkwright, Hutton, Hubbart, Brindley, Bramah, Leslie, Stevenson, Perkins, and Fulton. To these dozens of others might be added—among them Buffon, Davy, and Cuvier.

tries mentioned in the extract, custom of long standing has established the *belief*, that " the Greek and Roman classics constitute an essential part of a liberal education." This belief, however, does not form a fact. No mere belief does so. If it did, fact and absurdity would be often identical.

That at the time of the Revival of Letters, and for centuries afterwards, an acquaintance with the " Greek and Roman classics constituted an essential part of a liberal education," is not denied. The reason is obvious. At that period, those works were, in Europe and most parts of Asia, the depositories of almost all recorded knowledge. But they are not so now. The amount of knowledge which they lock up, at present, from the mere reader of modern languages, is extremely small, and, we may safely add, of little use. All the important information they contain has been long since translated into other tongues; hence they are no longer consulted as oracles of science. Had the Committee, therefore, pronounced a knowledge of them a *fashionable* or *conventional*, instead of an " essential," part of a liberal education, the term would have been more appropriate. If mere authority be waved, the propriety of the epithet, in the present condition of the world, is more than doubtful. But that authority is, in many cases, not only a fallacious, but a dangerous basis of education, may be easily shewn. Has not a belief in the infallibility of the Pope, in the performance of miracles by the relics of saints, and in the divine right of kings to trample on their subjects, been inculcated by authority as an element of education? And, in some parts of Europe, is it not so inculcated still? Has there not been a period when, had teachers refused to implant these notions in the minds of their pupils, they would have been deemed heretical, and deprived of their offices, if not of their lives? The reply to these questions must be affirmative. Were we inclined to press this matter further, we might add, that the time was, when no person but a clergyman was deemed sufficiently pure and holy to be at the head of a college or a university, because no other could procure for it the favour of heaven; and the time also was, when no young man's education was esteemed liberal and complete, though he might be intended for holy orders, unless it included the art of defence. In fact, there is scarcely an error or an absurdity in discipline so gross and striking as not to have found its advocacy in the same source. It is not perceived, then, in what way the committee have strengthened their cause, by a reference to fashion, or human authority. We shall appeal hereafter to a higher tribunal, that of Nature. The Committee employ another argument, the soundness of which we think equally doubtful. We shall give it in their own words:—

" The literature of every country of Europe is founded, more or less, on classical literature, and receives *from this source its most important illustrations.*"

Admitting this to be true of the literature of France, Italy, Spain, and Portugal, and also of modern Greece as far as she has a literature, is it so of that of any other European country? Is it true of Great Britain, Holland, Germany, Prussia, Russia, or any other northern nation? or is it true of the United States? Is the literature of these latter countries founded on that of ancient Greece or Rome? and is it dependent on " that source for its most important illustrations?" The Committee would hazard much in replying affirmatively to this question. In plain terms, if we comprehend their meaning in the paragraph quoted, the reply could not be sustained. The constitution of the English language, and every thing fundamental that belongs to it, rest much more on the Saxon than on either the Greek or Latin, or on both united; and the Russian, and the German in all its dialects, are original tongues,—no more dependent on the Greek or Latin than the latter are on them. That many English writers have modelled their style and manner after those of the writers of Greece and Rome, is true; but that the most pure and classical writers of the English language have done so, is not true. English literature has a character of its own, very distinct from that of either Greek or Roman literature. It cannot conform to both of them, they being widely different from each other. The truth is, that, when pure, it conforms to neither. This is proved by the prose works of Dryden, Bolingbroke, Swift, Addison, Taylor, Goldsmith, Scott, and other great masters of English style. Those compositions, and many others that might be referred to, derive nothing in manner or illustration from ancient literature, and but little in words. They are written chiefly in Saxon-English. We allude especially to the structure and spirit of the composition. Some of the most tasteless works in our language are modelled after the ancients. How can it be otherwise? An effort is made in them to assimilate incongruous things. Attempts, moreover, to imitate bespeak inferiority, and contribute to perpetuate it. On that ground, ancient authors have injured many modern ones. No writer will ever be great unless he aspire to originality, both in manner and matter. He must act according to the constitution of his own mind, not in imitation of the mind of another; for his intellectual stores, he must draw on nature; and, to acquire mental vigour and dexterity, he must exercise regularly, and on suitable subjects, the powers he possesses. But the adorers of the ancients will be the last to do this. Like the adherents to royalty, they will continue to recognise, in the Greeks and Romans, a *divine right* to instruct the moderns.

English literature will never attain the perfection of which it is susceptible, until it shall be cultivated, more than ever it has been, on the ground of the true constitution of the English tongue. Never until then will it be free from trammels; and freedom is essential to perfection in every thing. We deem it fortunate that this sentiment has begun to prevail; and that it has so begun cannot be doubted. English and American writers *generally* are less servile copyists of the ancients than they were fifty years ago; and, *as nations*, their writings have improved. Both in Great Britain and the United States, more especially in the latter, there are *twenty* good writers now, where there was *one* at the commencement of our revolutionary war; yet in neither country has the devotion to the ancient classics increased in the same ratio. It would be difficult to prove, that, in proportion to numbers, it has increased at all. Nor shall we ever have a truly classical literature of our own, until it shall have been formed out of our own materials, and on the constitution and construction of our own tongue. We might safely add, that when one writer copies or imitates the style and manner of another, he is apt to imitate his sentiments and mode of thinking also, and to become a copyist and an underling throughout; and such a degree of dependence operates as a blight on the human faculties. That it may be able to act with its entire force, and achieve every thing of which it is capable, the mind must be free, and must, therefore, do homage to nothing that is human. Aristotle and Plato among the ancients, and Newton and Locke among the moderns, checked originality of thought, and thus did mischief, through the excessive deference paid to them by their contemporaries and those of after ages. Imitation and the restraint of authority chill the fires and deaden the elasticity of genius, and are fatal to all that is great or new. We do not hesitate to say, then, that instead of being benefited by the homage once paid by them to ancient compositions, modern writers have improved, both in manner and style, almost in proportion as that homage has abated. As far as our acquaintance with German literature fits us to judge of it, we cannot perceive that it is any more "founded on classical literature" than the English. It appears to us to be very independent, and to have a distinct constitution and character of its own. To crowd a composition with what are called classical illustrations and allusions, is now deemed a mark of pedantry rather than of good taste; to which might be added, that it is also a mark of a barren mind. The rich are not compelled to borrow; nor is the scholar, who is sufficiently versed in the book of nature, obliged to rely for his illustrations on the literature of the ancients.

The Committee make a further effort to establish, *by analogy*, the high claim of an acquaintance with Greek and Latin to enter as an element into a liberal education. The subjects of their analogy are architecture and sculpture. Those arts are stated to have been carried to such perfection in Greece, that their products are still unrivalled, and constitute the best models for modern imitation. True; as relates to sculpture, the committee disclaim being advocates of *imitation*. To us, however, they seem to disclaim it only *in words*, while *in principle* they recommend it. When a modern statuary places an ancient bust or statue before him, and works *by* it or *after* it, to improve himself as an artist, we know of no other name which suits him so well as that of *imitator*. His object is not to *avoid faults* in the statue; because he always selects the most perfect specimen. If, then, he does not intend to imitate, to assimilate his work in some way to the model in his presence, why does he look on it as an exemplar? Why does he not copy directly from nature, the true inspirer of genius, and the finished pattern of all elegance and all excellence? By doing so, and depending alone on her, in conforming to her works, he would take the rank of an original. But as long as he relies for his improvement on human productions, he is a copyist. Every great artist has a *beau ideal* in his mind, the creation of his own genius; but all the elements of it are derived from nature. He only unites and fashions them to his taste; and, in his attempts to attain perfection, he works after the image he has thus created. His effort is to equal that, not to equal or surpass a pattern set by any other artist, either ancient or modern. After whose models did Phidias or Praxiteles work; or by what artist's productions did they improve themselves? The answer is plain. They worked after no models but those of Nature, and deigned to imitate no productions but her's,—and hence their works bestowed immortality on them. It is believed that the ancient artists, painters as well as sculptors, owed their excellence chiefly to their being *originals*. Nor could they be otherwise, because they had no highly finished works of preceding artists to imitate. Were the moderns to follow their examples of *originality*, instead of copying their works, they might equal them in the perfection of the art; but they will never do it on any other ground. It appears to us that the chief, if not the only advantage, which the works of ancient artists can bestow on modern ones, is on the ground of competition and rivalry. They may excite in them a higher ambition to excel than they would otherwise feel; and there, we apprehend, the true benefit ends. Our allusion is to artists of a high order. That inferior ones may improve their humble performances by imitation, is not denied. They are intended and fit only to follow in the wake of superior men. They are not, therefore, embraced in the present discussion. We are treating of artists qualified to be originals; and they are necessarily injured by imitation.

Be these things, however, as they may, we say of this analogy, as we did of the last, that it *proves* nothing, because it *is* an analogy, and not, we think, a very close one. In the reasoning founded on it by the Committee, the premises and the conclusions do not appear to us to belong of right to the same syllogism. Modern architecture, say the Committee, has been improved by ancient architecture, and modern sculpture by ancient sculpture. But the Greeks and Romans were the great masters in these arts. Therefore, modern literature is improved by ancient literature, in which the same people were also masters. We confess our inability to perceive either the force or fairness of the inference.

There is yet another ground on which the analogy of the Committee appears to us to have failed. Sculpture is a direct imitation of something in nature. The product, therefore, of the ancient and of the modern sculptor, when imitating the same object—say the human figure— must be so much alike, that the latter, when possessed of but moderate abilities, *may*, perhaps, improve his style by working after the model left by the former. He is still indirectly imitating nature, when he is imitating a well-executed image of her. But language, though founded in nature, resembles none of her immediate works. It is a creation entirely artificial; and, as products of art, the English, Latin, and Greek languages are, in their present condition, so dissimilar to each other, that it is difficult to conceive how the former can be in any way improved, by an attempt to model it after either of the latter. That it must be injured by it seems, on principle, the more probable result; and experience, we think, sustains the opinion.

" But (say the Committee) the study of the classics is useful, not only as it lays the *foundation of a correct taste*, and furnishes the student with *those elementary ideas* which are found in the literature of modern times, and which he *no where so well acquires as in their original sources*—but also as the study itself *forms the most effectual discipline of the mental faculties.*" * * * * " *Every faculty* of the mind *is employed;* not only the *memory, judgment,* and *reasoning powers,* but the *taste* and *fancy,* are occupied and improved."

The matter of this extract brings us into a more serious conflict with the Committee than that of either of the preceding ones. We are compelled to call in question the soundness of the whole of it. We cannot admit that " the study of the classics lays the foundation of a correct taste." Wherever that " *foundation*" exists, it is not the creation of any course of discipline. It is the gift of *nature*—laid in the original constitution of the mind. Education improves it, but does not and cannot *produce* it. There are many minds, some of whose powers are active and vigorous, in which no system of training can form a correct taste. Whatever they do is disjointed and out of shape; yet they may be thoroughly imbued with Greek and Latin. Instances in proof of this are so numerous, that they must be familiar to every accurate observer. The elements of correct taste are as literally bestowed by nature, as the elements of beauty of countenance or symmetry of figure. They consist in that form of mind where all the faculties are active and well balanced, none of them preponderating much in strength over the others. Where these elements are wanting no course of discipline can impart them; nor are we convinced that, when possessed, they may not be as well cultivated, without Greek and Latin, as with them. Females excel in all sorts of taste without any knowledge of ancient literature. This point will be more fully considered hereafter.

Notwithstanding an attentive examination of the subject, we find it difficult to discover what the Committee mean by " those elementary ideas, which are found in the literature of modern times, and which the student no where so well acquires as in their *original sources*." Nature,* not classical literature, we regard as the " *original* source" of all ideas, whether elementary or of any other kind. We believe, moreover, that all mental philosophers concur with us in opinion. Other sources are but secondary, and derive all the value they possess from their conformity to the original source; but Nature is as accessible to the moderns as she was to the ancients. Had we said that she is much more so, the position could be maintained: for each well-informed student of nature possessed by Greece and Rome, modern nations furnish hundreds in the same amount of population. Wherefore, then, must the latter depend on the former for " elementary ideas," or any ideas at all, to enrich their literature? Why can they not draw them from the same fountain, which is so much more liberally open to the modern than it was to the ancient world? We ought rather to ask, Do they not thus draw them? Are not modern productions generally much richer in the truths of nature, and freer from fiction, than most ancient ones? This question must be answered affirmatively, else all the discoverers and philosophers, who have flourished and written since the revival of letters, have

---

* We mean that impressions made, directly or indirectly, by the works of nature, on the human mind, produce in it all the ideas it possesses. To the production of these impressions, the learned languages contribute but little.

lived in vain. We feel justified, then, in calling on the Committee to specify those " elementary ideas," and show them to be of any value, which writers of the present day most readily derive from Greek and Latin. Nor will they find it an easy task to comply with the summons.

We cannot concur in the opinion that the study of the dead languages " forms the most effectual discipline of the mental faculties"—especially of " judgment and the reasoning powers." On the contrary, we are convinced that it does not. We do not perceive how it disciplines either " reason" or " judgment" at all. Nor do we think it does so. Some of the most thorough-bred Hellenists and Latinists we have seen were eminently defective in reason and judgment. Nor is this an uncommon occurrence. Observation has taught us to believe the reverse. We think it rare to find, in our colleges and elsewhere, that those young men, who judge most correctly, reason most conclusively, compose most elegantly, and debate most eloquently and powerfully, are most perfectly versed in the ancient languages. And if the study of Greek and Latin invigorates the " memory," it is a memory for *words*, not for *ideas* of qualities, objects, events, or *their relations*. And the cultivation of a modern tongue will have the same effect. The reason of all this is obvious. The cultivation of Greek and Latin is but the study of words in one language, and their synonymes or representatives in another. It does not, therefore, and cannot strengthen the memory for any thing but language; and, we repeat, that that form of memory can be strengthened as well by the study of English and French, as of Greek and Latin.

The chief source of error on this topic is the belief that memory is a *faculty* of the mind, and that we have but *one* kind of memory; whereas it is but a *function* or *mode of operation* of a faculty. We have, therefore, as many sorts of memory as the mind possesses of intellectual faculties, each faculty having its own; and as no one primitive faculty can form the ideas which are the product of another, neither can it remember them, because it never had them. Memory is the power of recalling ideas which were once possessed. The cultivation of the memory belonging to one faculty of the mind, then, does not strengthen the memory belonging to another, any more than the cultivation of hearing strengthens vision, or of smelling, touch. To illustrate this by examples.

The mind possesses one faculty for number, which can perceive and remember nothing but number; another for form or figure, which perceives and remembers nothing but figure; another for size; another for place; another for colour; another for time, and another for tune; and each perceives and remembers only the class of ideas proper to itself. In cultivating any one of these faculties, therefore, by exercising it on the objects which especially suit it, its own memory is strengthened; but no strength is added to the memory of any other faculty.*

* We might thus enumerate all the intellectual faculties, and show that they are acted on and exercised only each by objects or agents proper to itself; that each forms and remembers only its own class of ideas; and that, therefore, the cultivation of one of them does not improve *directly* the functions of another. That it may receive strength and become dexterous in action, each one must be exercised in its own line. The faculties of Individuality and Eventuality must be exercised on single objects and events, Comparison chiefly on the relations of analogy, and Causality on those of cause and effect.

Respecting the *animal* and *moral* faculties, the same is true. Each one of them is exercised and strengthened only by its own objects, and in its own way. The proper education of each, therefore, is specific, and contributes nothing directly to the education of another.

It is in the education of the moral faculties that the teachers of youth are most deficient. They seem to think that they are improving their pupils in morality, when they are merely restraining them from vice. Nothing, however, can be more erroneous. The teaching of morality is as much a *positive* process, as teaching to read and write. The moral faculties, we mean, must be actively exercised, each on its proper object. The faculty of Benevolence is strengthened only by the work of benevolence, and the contemplation of kind actions. The faculty of Conscientiousness is strengthened by contemplating and doing what is just and right. The faculty of Veneration delights in doing homage to superior beings, and derives from the practice its chief improvement.

The mind possesses a faculty for language, by the cultivation of which *its* memory is in like manner strengthened; but, as already mentioned, that is only memory for *words*. No new strength is added to the memory for any other classes of ideas. Hence the well-known fact, that different individuals excel in different forms of memory. One remembers *numbers* with great tenacity, Ideality is exercised and strengthened by beauty and sublimity, and Firmness gains power from scenes of difficulty.

Of the animal faculties the same may be affirmed. Combativeness is strengthened by a familiarity with danger, Acquisitiveness by the pursuit of wealth, and Destructiveness by cruelty and the shedding of blood.

We shall only add, that, so perfectly do the faculties of the mind harmonize with the works of creation, that each finds, abundantly, suitable objects for its own exercise, enjoyment, and increase in strength. Nor will instructors ever be competent to their duty, until they realise this truth, and act in conformity to it.

As relates to the cultivation of the *moral faculties*, no one will contend that that is highly promoted by the study of Greek and Latin. It may, at least, be questioned, whether it is promoted at all. Many have believed the reverse to be true. That some striking examples of morality, especially as respects certain virtues, are exhibited in the ancient classics, is not denied. But the scale of immorality greatly preponderates. The entire scheme of the Greek and Roman mythology, is a revolting picture of licentiousness and crime. Jupiter, at once the chief of gods and adulterers. Apollo, the gallant, gay Lothario of heaven and earth. Mars, a blood-thirsty, swaggering bully. Neptune, a blustering boaster, and a flagrant ravisher. Vulcan, a low-bred, deformed, ill-tongued ruffian. Bacchus, a sot. Juno, a fierce, vindictive termagant. Minerva, a prude; and most of the other female divinities *no better than they ought to be.*

Of the demi-gods and heroes, not one exhibits an example to be followed. Even the " pious Æneas, the goddess-born," was an ungrateful seducer, a lawless usurper, and an inexorable murderer.

Nor did the characters of the philosophers of either Greece or Rome approach immaculacy. Pericles waging a bloody war on account of his mistress, Socrates at the feet of Aspasia, and Cato accommodating a friend with his wife, are but sorry samples of morality for modern youth to imitate.

Nor is this all. In Horace, Ovid, Juvenal, Catullus, Anacreon, and other classical writers, are many odes, epistles, satires, and letters, too obscene for young men to read. In fine, if we would strengthen the moral faculties, and preserve their purity, we must exercise them in some other and better way than by the study of Greek and Latin.

but forgets a tune the moment the notes of it have escaped from his ear. Another never forgets a *tune*, after once hearing it, but cannot remember numbers. A third forgets both the tune and the number of times he has heard it, but remembers the *form* of the instrument on which it was played. A fourth forgets the tune, the number, and the figure of the instrument, but has an accurate recollection of the *place* where he heard the tune, and of the *person* who performed it. A fifth, forgetting all those things, remembers the *names* of the tunes, the instrument, and the musician. The latter is well endowed with the faculty of language, by the cultivation of which its own memory alone is improved—not, we repeat, the memory for any other class of ideas. As soon, therefore, shall a youth perfect himself in the dead languages by studying arithmetic or mathematics, as strengthen his memory for numbers or quantity by contracting an acquaintance with the ancient classics. Nor is it perceived in what way *taste* and *fancy* are more effectually exercised and improved by the study of ancient than of modern literature. We are even compelled to believe that they are not so. Many modern works might be mentioned which surpass any ancient ones now extant, in imagination and fancy. We know of no Greek or Roman authors equal, in these respects, to Shakspeare, Spencer, or Dante. Certainly none are superior. To come down to our own times, and compare moderns and ancients individually with each other, we think Byron superior in brilliancy to Pindar, and Moore to Anacreon. That they at least equal them, no one, we think, will deny; and that the moderns referred to are richer in sentiment and thought than the ancients, will not, we apprehend, be held doubtful. Nor are they inferior in taste when they choose to exercise it. Yet their works are original—no more founded on, or modelled after, the works of any of the ancients, than the latter are after them. They are the productions of the peculiar geniuses of their authors, and resemble nothing but themselves.

That it may be further illustrated and confirmed, we repeat a remark already made, that no faculty of the mind but that of language is especially disciplined by the study of Greek and Latin. Hence persons who are deficient in that faculty make but little progress in this study, however industrious they may be, and though their other faculties may be unusually strong and active. Many striking instances of this are on record; and most persons must have seen some such themselves. Great as were their powers in other respects, neither Newton nor Swift could acquire any standing in classical scholarship. The reason is plain. They were comparatively defective in the faculty of Language. Mere boys, on the contrary, who are highly endowed with it, but whose reason and judgment are immature and weak, make rapid progress in the classics. As relates to that branch of attainment, the maturity of the higher faculties of the mind is of little avail. We once knew a child but six years old who spoke four different languages; and lads of ten frequently surpass youths of eighteen or twenty, in the ease and speed with which they become acquainted with Greek and Latin. Many persons, who acquire distinction as classical scholars, can never attain a name in science.

Shall we be told, that it is not by learning to construe, parse, and scan the ancient languages, that the faculties of pupils are exercised and strengthened, but by studying their structure and philosophy? We reply, that the number of persons who study Greek and Latin thus thoroughly, is very small; and, were it otherwise, an equal degree of improvement might be derived from a suitable attention to the structure and philosophy of modern languages. There are reasons why the case cannot be otherwise. The philosophy, by which we mean the reason and fundamental principles, of all languages is the same. A brief analysis of the subject will prove this.

From their social character and love of information, mankind have an irrepressible desire to communicate to their fellows something respecting themselves, and to learn something respecting others; and words are the chief means by which these ends are obtained. Language, then, might be defined an invention for expressing, by articulate sounds, the feelings, operations, and states of the mind, the influences produced on it by the objects and events of the external world, and the relations of those objects and events to each other, as they appear to the mental eye.

In all nations the faculties of the mind are the same, differing only in degree; and the external world, with its leading objects and occurrences, and their relations both to the mind and to each other, are also the same. Hence the feelings, operations, and states of the mind are, in kind, likewise identical. It follows, therefore, of necessity, that the fundamental principles of the means of expressing these things are in like manner identical. A brief detail will illustrate this, as far as is requisite to our present purpose.

The external world consists of substances or objects, with their qualities and relations, and the movements or changes by which those qualities and relations are altered. The changes are called events. Out of this state of things arise the three principal parts of speech, which are necessarily the same in every language; the *noun substantive*, being the name of objects or events; the *adjective*, denoting their qualities; and the *verb*, which expresses the chief relations and their changes. The latter part of speech expresses also simple existence. In every change of quality or relation produced, some object must act, and others be acted on. Hence arise two forms of the verb, the *active* and *passive;* and two cases or conditions of the noun, the nominative and objective. When action is represented as passing from one substance or thing to another, that which performs the action is in the nominative case, and that which sustains it is in the objective. By the passive form of the verb, action is expressed as falling on some object or thing, without any necessary reference to the source from which it comes. The recipient of the action is then in the nominative or objective case, according to the mode of expression used.

Nouns have also other cases or conditions, which are represented in some languages by changes or inflections in the terminations of the nouns themselves, and, in others, by certain words accompanying them.

Actions or events occur at different times, and under different circumstances and relations. These also the verb must express. Hence the different tenses, referring to periods past, present, and to come; and the different moods, denoting the manner and circumstances of the action. Both moods and tenses are formed, in some instances, by changes in the terminations of the verb, and, in others, by means of auxiliary verbs. Languages differ considerably in the precision with which they mark the relative dates of past and future events; and no little of the perfection of the language depends on this. Another variety in forms of expression is rendered necessary by the different numbers of the things that act, and of those that are acted on. This end is attained by the singular, dual, and plural numbers of nouns and verbs. Concord and government between words are also essential attributes of language.

The frequent repetition of nouns or the names of things in discourse or writing would be not only ungraceful but inconvenient. Hence the formation of *pronouns*, or words serving as substitutes for nouns. Actions have qualities as well as objects; and it is necessary that they also be expressed in speech. This end is attained by the formation of *adverbs*. Between both objects and actions there are certain minute relations and connexions, which cannot be represented by verbs. This want is supplied by *prepositions* and *conjunctions*. There are instinctive exclamations, expressive of certain internal feelings; as those of joy, sorrow, surprise, affright, and others. From this source have arisen the vocables called *interjections*. The last part of speech to be mentioned is the *participle*; so called, because, in form and meaning, it partakes of both the verb and the noun, especially the noun-adjective. By contributing to accuracy and completeness of expression, it is highly useful in speech. The qualities of objects and actions often differ in degree. To meet this want, the different degrees of comparison are instituted. Objects also differ in sex. Corresponding to this, nouns have different genders, which, in different languages, are marked in different ways.

The impressions made directly and primitively on the mind, by the objects and events of the external world, excite ideas of simple perception. These are expressed by their appropriate nouns, as colour, sound, form, size, resistance, place, storm, battle. So are the objects which produce them; as grass, tree, horse, man, mountain, trumpet, army, air, cloud. These simple ideas, formed by the perceptive faculties, constitute the elements of knowledge. By working on them, through its reflecting faculties, which are of a higher order, and which operate each according to its nature, the mind forms from them other ideas of a more complex, subtle, and abstract character. To represent these, corresponding nouns or names are invented, and make a part of language. Some of these are as follows: like, unlike, likeness, unlikeness, difference, identity, whiteness, blackness, virtue, vice, right, wrong, cause, effect, and many others. The formation of abstract ideas being one of the highest operations of the mind, the existence of the abstract terms, by which they are expressed, gives evidence of a corresponding degree of perfection in speech. Hence rude and ignorant nations have but few abstractions.

Inasmuch, then, as language not only presents a picture of the external world as it appears to the mind, but gives also a representation of the various faculties of the mind, of their present condition, and of the degree of their general discipline and the extent of their operations, it follows, that its copiousness and perfection must correspond to the mental cultivation of the people who speak it. In plainer terms, the richer a people are in knowledge, the more numerous and abstract are their ideas, and the more copious, refined, and perfect is their language. While this influence is deducible from first principles, its truth is established by observation. Nor will it be denied, that the more perfect and copious a language is, the more invigorating and improving is the exercise which the study of its structure and philosophy affords to the mind. Much of the mental discipline imparted by this exercise arises from the investigation of *concord, government*, and *structure;* and they are common to every language.

The correctness of the foregoing principles, generally, will not be controverted. Suppose, then, a comparison, in conformity to them, be instituted between the Greek or the Latin, and the English languages; which of them will preponderate, as a philosophical study? Will the English be found inferior to the others? No colour of reason is perceived for thinking so, but rather the reverse. Its fundamental principles are the same, its structure is as good, and its superior copiousness is striking. Nor is it inferior in force, correctness, variety, precision, or elegance of expression. If the faculties of pupils are at any time more severely exercised in studying Greek or Latin than in studying English or French, it is because they are more *puzzled* to detect the meaning of the former than of the latter. But such puzzling is neither pleasant nor instructive. On the contrary, it fatigues the mind without improving it, and often produces an aversion from learning. All things considered, we feel convinced, that no mental faculty is disciplined and strengthened by studying Greek and Latin, which may not be as profitably trained, and as highly invigorated, by the study of English and French, provided it be pursued in a judicious manner, and to the requisite extent. The misfortune is, and we might add the *fault* is, that in most colleges in the United States, where *days* are devoted to the cultivation of a knowledge of the ancient languages, *hours* are not given to the *real study* of our mother tongue. To read a few books at times very loosely, and scarcely ever critically, and write a few formal exercises in English, is not the way to become versed, as every educated American ought to be, in the English language. It is not the way to *study* it, and gain a philosophical knowledge and a full command of it in writing and speaking. Yet, in most of our seats of learning, but little more is done to ripen English scholars. We are acquainted with no institution, whether academy, college, or university, where the pupils are thoroughly disciplined in English—none where they are called on to master it completely as a branch of philosophy, and reduce their knowledge of it to practice, by sufficient training in composition and rhetoric. We know that no such institution exists in the *United States;* and we *believe* that none such exists in *Great Britain.* The result is often manifested by literary wants, peculiarly discreditable to our systems of instruction. We have seen many college graduates, who could translate Greek and Latin with considerable fluency, and even write and converse in them, whose knowledge of English literature was so radically defective, that they could not compose a decent letter. Their deficiency was striking even in the spelling of common words. We could name an individual, who has been a *Professor* in *one* college, and a *President elect* of *three* others, if not *four*, of whom this is true! He is ignorant alike of the construction and orthography of his mother-tongue! And yet he is a Greek and Latin scholar! On the contrary, many a boarding-school girl, who is a stranger to ancient literature, speaks and writes the English language with fluency and correctness. Why? because she has been exercised in it—the only way in which a true knowledge and practical command of it can ever be acquired; and it can be thus acquired, without a knowledge of any other language.*

* It cannot be denied, that, in one respect at least, the study of Greek and Latin has been injurious. It has prevented the actual and thorough study of English. The ground on which it has done this is obvious. Latin and Greek are the ancient and classical, and therefore reputedly the superior languages. A knowledge of them, therefore, is comparatively an object of high ambition. Hence, they are *studied*. Not so with English. It is a modern, every-day language, a knowledge of which is neither an object of ambition, nor a point of honour or pride. Hence, instead of being *studied*, it is simply *read*. And, while the ancient languages are taught by men of talents and cultivation, in handsome and even magnificent edifices, it is *pretended* to

The writings of the ancients have long ceased to be a source of *science*. All their most valuable *historical matter* is also translated into some of the living languages, especially into English. It has been shewn, moreover, that the study of them does not give to the faculties of the pupil a degree of exercise more improving than the thorough study of a modern tongue. Whatever advantages, then, may result from a knowledge of the ancient classics, belong to literature alone. Science, we say, disclaims them. Shall we be told that an acquaintance with them prepares the mind better for the reception of science, general and professional, than any other sort of attainment? The friends of this notion, long as it has prevailed, and almost universal as it is, ought not to be surprised if, on being placed in the balance, it should be found wanting. But, before weighing it, we must examine one or two other arguments, urged by the Committee, in favour of the study of Greek and Latin. When speaking of the study of modern languages, they say:—

" If the languages and literature of Italy, France, and Spain, beyond what is merely superficial, are an object with the student, they should be acquired *through the Latin;*

be taught in log cabins, by men who are ignorant of it, and of every thing else. We repeat, without fear of being put in the wrong, that this neglect of English, and the low estimation in which the study of it is held by the public, is to be attributed chiefly to the attachment of too much importance to an acquaintance with Greek and Latin.

True, this state of things is passing away, and may it pass speedily! The change within the present century is great, and all for the better. In most, we believe in all the respectable seats of learning in our country, the cultivation of the English language is improving. Still, however, it is every where much below what it ought to be, and what we trust it will be by the middle of the century. We shall only add, that those whose native tongue is English, should make it a point of national pride and ambition, not only to understand it thoroughly, but to give it a high standing, in the estimation of the world, to which it is entitled. And this can be done only by making it a subject of serious study. That being effected, English will be no longer a *step-child* in our academies, colleges, and universities. The ancient languages will be no longer permitted to overshadow it, and triumph in its degradation.

nor is there reason to doubt, so far as experience affords the means of judging, that it is the most *expeditious* mode of acquiring a familiarity with the languages in question."

In the sentiment here advanced we cannot concur. Reason, observation, experience, and every other consideration bearing on it, unite in persuading us that it is unfounded. We acknowledge the close family-alliance between Latin, Italian, French, and Spanish, the former being the parent-tongue. But we *know* that, by the adoption and steady pursuit of the proper course, a " familiarity" with the *three last* can be acquired, not only without the aid of the *first*, but in a *period not longer, if so long*, as that requisite to the attainment of a similar "*familiarity*" with the *first alone*. Latin, as usually studied, cannot be mastered in less than three years. Few students can become really " familiar" with it even in that time. Yet, in the same period, a youth of common capacity may become so well versed in Italian, French, and Spanish, as to speak and write them with fluency and correctness. We say this *can* be done, because we know it has been done. Might we speak of our personal experience, we would say, that we knew something of Latin when we studied the modern tongues; yet we were insensible of any facilities derived from the attainment; except as related to our knowledge of *language in the abstract*, and some experience and *tact* we had gained in learning it; and that might have been acquired from the study of *any language*—we mean the study of it *philosophically*. Some of our fellow-students, who had no knowledge of Latin, and who were not accounted more apt than ourselves in learning languages, formed an acquaintance with French, Italian, and Spanish, very near as readily as we did, and seemed, in a short time, to understand them as thoroughly. We believe some of the best French and Italian teachers in the United States, prefer that their pupils *should not have learned Latin*. The female academies in our country furnish a strong argument in support of our views on this subject. Their pupils are strangers to Latin; yet they learn French and

Italian with more facility, and as much accuracy, as most of our youths at college.

When about to advance the sentiment we are now considering, the Committee would have done well to have remembered the law maxim, *Quod probat nimis, probat nihil.* They certainly attempted to prove too much in favour of classical learning, when they asserted, that the attainment of a knowledge of it is " the most *expeditious* mode of acquiring a familiarity with Italian, French, and Spanish"—thus alleging, if we understand their meaning, that a youth can attain a knowledge of Latin and French, Latin and Italian, or Latin and Spanish, in a shorter time than he can learn either of the three modern languages alone! We shall only add, that scores of individuals might be named, who, without having ever looked into a Latin author, have acquired a knowledge of " the languages and literature of Italy, France, and Spain," *far* " *beyond what is merely superficial.*" Can a foreigner— say a Frenchman or German—attain, through a familiarity with Greek and Latin, a more thorough and commanding knowledge of English, than an American or an Englishman can, without Greek and Latin, but completely disciplined in his native tongue? An affirmative answer to this question would be alike inconsistent with reason and experience. Nor can an American acquire, by the aid of Latin, as perfect an acquaintance with French, as a Parisian can without it. One extract more, and we shall have done with the pamphlet.

" We are the people (say the Committee), the genius of whose government and institutions, more especially and imperiously than any other, demands that the field of classical learning be industriously and thoroughly explored and cultivated, and its rich productions gathered. The models of ancient literature, which are put into the hands of the young student, can hardly fail to imbue his mind with the principles of liberty; to inspire the liveliest patriotism, and to excite to noble and generous action, and are therefore peculiarly adapted to the American youth. To appreciate justly the character of the ancients, the thorough study and accurate knowledge of their classics, in the language of the originals, is indispensable; as the simplicity, energy, and striking peculiarities of these pristine exemplars of freedom, which are forcibly and beautifully displayed in their models of classical literature, are scarcely more discoverable in ordinary or even the most faithful translations, than are the warmth, animation, and intellectual illumination of the living, active, and intelligent being, in the sculptured imitation of the statuary."

This is the most exceptionable paragraph we have quoted. It has much more of rant than reason in it. Some people will call it eloquent; and its author perhaps intended to make it so. We call it declamatory, frothy, and erroneous; while plainness, solidity, and truth are essential to eloquence. It is a tissue of assertion, unsupported by a tittle of proof. It is equally extravagant in language and sentiment. Who ever dreamed before of deriving from the writings of the ancients, either sparks to kindle, or breath to fan, the fires of freedom and patriotism in modern bosoms? As well might the fancy have been indulged of brightening and swelling the blaze of Moscow by a farthing rush-light, when the conflagration was at its height. We venture to say, that for *every single paragraph* breathing a spirit of *rational freedom*, that can be found in the literature of Greece and Rome, *one thousand* are contained in the works of British, American, and other modern writers. Nor, on this subject, did the moderns borrow from the ancients. The reason is plain. The latter had little or nothing to lend. The former, therefore, looked into themselves, and into the reason and nature of things, and found *there* the treasures they sought. And, as to patriotism, the uncultured Caledonians of old, and the Swiss peasants at a later period, displayed as much of it as ever the Greeks or Romans did. And so would the uncultured Irish now, were they in a condition to do so. Was it ancient literature that taught and emboldened the barons of England to extort from their monarch their Magna Charta? No: such was their want of scholarship, that they could scarcely read the instrument, when prepared. Some of them could not read at all. Yet that single charter contains more of the genuine principles of freedom and human rights, than all that the Greeks and Romans could boast. Were the American patriots better versed in ancient literature than any other people, when they asserted and achieved their independence? Many who had never opened a Latin dictionary, and who were strangers to the Greek alphabet, acted distinguished parts on that occasion. Be the cause what it may, the Anglo-Saxons and their descendants have long understood, and understand at present, what salutary freedom is, much better than any other people. The Greeks and Romans might have derived useful lessons from them on that subject. Nor is it true that a spirit of freedom and patriotism has prevailed in European countries, in proportion to the prevalence of classical knowledge. We do not say that the reverse of this is true—though facts somewhat favourable to such a position might be adduced; but we do say, that it is a knowledge of *nature*, not of Greek and Latin, which teaches man his rights.* We shall only add, that in the Mississippi Valley, where classical literature has not yet taken root, the spirit of patriotism is as pure and pervasive, and the love and knowledge of freedom as fer-

---

* There is a much greater amount of classical learning in Germany, than in any other equal portion of the globe. Why, then, have not the Germans taken a lead in the overthrow of despotism, the assertion of human right, and the establishment of freedom? Why, on the contrary, do they calmly tolerate the sway of one of the most despotic governments of Europe? The reason is plain. The spirit of freedom is awakened and nourished, not by the classical tomes of the ancients, but by the books of the moderns—more especially, however, by the book of Nature. That chapter of the latter, which gives the true history and philosophy of man, his rights, privileges, and all his relations, contains a hundred-fold more of the spirit of freedom, than all the Greeks and Romans ever wrote. Let the Germans study that, with but half the attention they bestow on ancient literature, and the Austrian and Prussian sceptres will soon be shorn of much of their power, or shattered to pieces.

vid and correct, as in any other portion of the globe—much more so than they ever were in Greece or Rome.

Nor can we subscribe to the belief, however general, and however often and dogmatically asserted, that it is impossible to infuse into an English translation the spirit, force, and fire of an ancient Greek or Roman composition. Or, if an impossibility of the kind exist, it is because the original production is not fully comprehended and felt. And if the disciplined translator cannot become thoroughly master of the original, is it probable that the common reader of Greek and Latin can? If the better scholar fail, will the worse succeed? These questions answer themselves.

The English is as powerful and expressive a language as the Latin or Greek; and, as heretofore mentioned, it is more copious than either. It is in vain to tell us, then, that when an Englishman or an American fully comprehends the meaning, and enters perfectly into the spirit, of a piece of ancient literature, whether it be prose or verse, and is, at the same time, equal as a writer to the author of it—and practice will render him so—it is in vain, we say, to contend that, under these circumstances, a translation may not be rendered equal to the original. If, owing to the peculiarities of different languages, some transient beauties be lost, others may be added, and neither the meaning nor the spirit of the ancient composition be marred. In proof of this, we offer Murphy's translation of Tacitus, in which we venture to say there are but few if any passages where the Roman historian and biographer has suffered in the version. In some, we have thought him improved. Nor do we hesitate to add, that there is not *one* Greek scholar in a *thousand*, who, did pride permit him to acknowledge the truth, does not read to more advantage, and with a higher relish, Pope's translation, than Homer's original. The same is true of the translation, by the same English author, of Ovid's celebrated letter of Sappho to Phaon. In spirit, feeling, and force, the translator has surpassed his original. True, he does not equal him in brevity of expression; nor, for reasons connected with the two languages, is it possible to render an

English translation as brief as a Latin original. But this is the only quality in which it need be inferior, and it is of but little moment. We shall only add, that the more purely and elegantly one language is written, the more easily and literally can it be translated into another. Hence the great facility of turning the writings of Voltaire into English.

We are aware of the prejudice arrayed against us on this subject. But we are unmoved by it, and fearlessly state what we believe, in defiance of it. We therefore repeat, that an English scholar, who is an able and accomplished writer, can, provided he thoroughly comprehends it and feels it, translate a Greek or Latin composition, matter and spirit, into his mother-tongue. And, unless the scholar who reads it in the original, thus comprehends and feels it, he does not enjoy it, and is not benefited by it, as the Committee allege he is. What advantage does he derive from visions of beauty floating in his mind, which he is unable to express in his own tongue? They neither enrich, strengthen, nor refine him, as a writer or a speaker. They are mere mental lumber, and therefore unavailable, if not prejudicial. But the truth is, that the whole matter is but a fancy. Whatever a scholar clearly understands, no matter from what source it is derived—the study of Greek and Latin, or the study of nature—he *can* communicate *clearly* and *forcibly*, provided he is a forcible thinker, and has made himself master of his native language. In contending, then, that an individual can be delighted and benefited by the beauties of works written in the dead languages, while he is unable to transfer those beauties, and use them in a living language, the Committee appear to us to have contradicted themselves. In such a case, there is no *delight* or *improvement*, without *actual possession* of what delights or improves; and, if *possessed*, the beauty can be translated, to delight and improve others.*

---

* It would be well for those who believe in the incommunicable beauties and delights inherent in Greek and Latin composition, to en-

To us, the opinion of the Committee seems equally unfounded, when they assert that, " to appreciate justly the character of the ancients, the thorough study and acdeavour to ascertain how much of those qualities are in the *sentiment,* and how much in the *sound.* The sonorousness and euphony of Greek and Latin are much superior to those of English. Of this, every classical scholar must be sensible. Hence much of the delight derived from reading them, is the delight of harmonious musical sound—especially when the sound is an " echo to the sense." We say " harmonious sound ;" for such is generally the exquisite order and arrangement of the words, that, if they be altered, much of the beauty of the passage is marred, and an equal amount of the pleasure of reading it dissipated. This may be illustrated and proved by the following quotations :—

" *Exoritur clamorque virûm clangorque tubarum*"—an exquisitely beautiful line, the sound fairly echoing the sense. Let the words be transposed into their natural order, " *Clamorque virûm clangorque tubarum exoritur,*" and more than half the beauty is gone.

" *Stat sonipes, ac fræna ferox spumantia mandit.*"
" *Ferox sonipes stat, ac mandit spumantia fræna.*"
" *Intonuere poli et crebris micat ignibus æther.*"
" *Poli intonuere et æther micat crebris ignibus.*"

Every one must perceive that the beauty of the two latter lines is equally destroyed, by changing the artificial into the natural arrangement of their words. Of Greek and Latin composition generally the same is true. The only object of transposition in it, is euphony and harmony, or the improvement of sound. In English composition, much is already done, and more *may* be done, in the same way.

There is also a reason, why we fancy more beauty in Greek and Latin composition, than we really *perceive.* We do not in general *perfectly understand* it. A sort of shadowy dimness hangs over its meaning. And every one knows that a little obscurity heightens materially the feeling of beauty and sublimity. This it does, by giving more play and wider scope to the imagination. The beauty of a moonlight scene is much improved by the fleecy rack which flits across the heavens.

Once more. Classical scholars are proud of their attainments. They, therefore, feel a selfish enjoyment in persuading themselves that they have access to rich fountains of pleasure, in their knowledge of Greek and Latin, from which the uninitiated are excluded. And it is a law of human nature, that men can so far realize their wishes, as to believe ultimately what they are anxious to believe. Such are some of the chief reasons why it is contended that the beauty and spirit of Greek and Latin composition are necessarily lost in a translation.

curate knowledge of their classics, in the language of the originals, are indispensable." The mere knowledge of a language, and of the number, form, and powers of the letters in which it is written, give but a very limited acquaintance with those who speak it. It is the literature and the history of a people that disclose their character. And, as respects the ancients, access can now be had to these two sources of information, without a knowledge of their language. We know of no Greek or Roman work, valuable on account of the matter it contains, which has not been translated. And, indeed, not a few have been translated, that have no intrinsic value. To call them curious, is to give them their full meed of praise. There is enough written in English, or translated into it, to communicate to those who will study it correctly, as intimate an acquaintance with the ancients, in every matter and relation worth knowing, as the most accomplished Hellenists and Latinists of the day have. To contend, then, that to gain a knowledge of the Greeks or Romans, in their manners, persons, customs, civil and household economy, or any thing else of moment, we must study their languages, is a mistake. As well may it be said, that, to attain a knowledge of the Russians or Laplanders, we must study *their* languages, instead of reading well-written histories of them. Some of the best-informed Grecian and Roman antiquarians we have seen, knew nothing of the dead languages. They had derived all their knowledge of antiquity from English publications, original or translated. Shakspeare, though unversed in the languages of the Greeks and Romans, had an intimate acquaintance with their characters, customs, manners, and literature. Yet, since his time, translations have been greatly multiplied and extended, and original works on those points written; and hence the same amount of knowledge which he had, may now be much more easily acquired.

The ancient languages, then, being no longer a source of either science or history, and the study of them having no more influence in training and strengthening the higher faculties of the mind than the study of modern languages, were the question put, " In what respect are scholars benefited by a knowledge of them ?" the answer must be, " In *polite literature* alone."* How far they are benefited even *there*, shall be our next inquiry. This brings us *to consider* a question proposed *in substance* in an early part of this article.

Can an Englishman or an American, versed in modern languages only—say English, French, and Italian—but thoroughly disciplined in science, become as able and accomplished a writer and speaker, as if he had a knowledge of Greek and Latin ?

This is an important problem, in the present state of the world—more especially, perhaps, in our own country; and we repeat, that it can be solved conclusively only by an experiment which has never yet been made. The effect of a true *modern education* has never been tried—certainly never on a broad scale. No one, we mean, as far as we are informed, has been thoroughly imbued with modern languages and modern science,† and

---

* It is urged by the Committee, as another argument in favour of a knowledge of Greek and Latin, that it qualifies its possessor better than he could be without it, to travel, for information or pleasure, through Europe. To this we shall only reply, that we have never found it necessary to converse in either Greek or Latin, in Europe, any more than in the United States. We have mingled somewhat there in literary and scientific society, as well as in social and fashionable circles; and English, French, or Italian, never failed to serve us as a medium of conversation. Through one or another of these languages, we could communicate intelligibly all we had to impart, and receive, in return, all we wished to know. And we believe the same is true of every other traveller, who mixes only in enlightened society. True, we met, *by accident*, a few bevies of *scholastics*, who manifested at once their learning and pedantry—not to say their ill-breeding—by speaking Latin, garnished occasionally with a scrap or two of Greek. But for such coteries we had no predilection, inasmuch as we usually found their *knowledge* of *ancient* affairs fully counterbalanced by their *ignorance* of *modern* ones—the latter being, in our opinion, the more important.

† Under the phrase " modern science," it will be understood that

extensively practised in writing and speaking, without having some acquaintance also with Greek and Latin. Hence a vast majority of great authors and orators have been necessarily more or less of classical scholars. It would be strange were it otherwise. The tide of opinion, united to the influence of *fashion*, has compelled every one educated for professional, public, or literary life, to pay some attention to ancient literature. But has this study aided them essentially in the attainment of distinction? or has it been only an accompaniment of it—tending, perhaps, to decorate the mind, but neither to enrich nor strengthen it? To reply, that it has been an indispensable element of the greatness and lustre acquired, would be hazardous, we think, for various reasons.

Some of the most distinguished orators of modern times have had but a slight acquaintance with Greek and Latin, and others none at all. Among the former may be mentioned Chatham, Erskine, and Hamilton; and among the latter, Henry, Whitefield, and two or three Americans now living, whom it might be indelicate to name. Respecting authors the same is true.

Shakspeare, the first writer, in some respects, the world has produced, was a stranger to the ancient languages; and Moliere, Fielding, and Cuvier were in the same condition. So was Franklin, whose style is a model of simplicity, perspicuity, and chasteness; and so was Washington, who wrote with uncommon elegance and power. Sir Humphrey Davy, an excellent writer, an eloquent speaker, President of the Royal Society, and the ablest chemist of his day, had no classical learning. We believe the same is true of Mr Bowditch, one of the most accomplished mathematicians and astronomers of the age, and an able writer; and we know the same was true of the late Mr Rittenhouse. Yet so deeply versed in astronomy was the latter, that, in the accuracy and import-

---

we include mathematics, and such other branches of science as were known to the ancients, with their modern improvements.

ance of his observations on the transit of Venus over the Sun, many years ago, he surpassed all the astronomers of Europe; and, in a mere literary point of view, some of his writings are highly creditable. Yet none of these studied English as thoroughly, or obtained as perfect a command of it, as he might have done. Each of them, therefore, might have greatly improved his style and manner as a writer, by a steady and continued effort to that effect.

That the style of English authors is far from being perfect in proportion to their knowledge of the dead languages, appears from numerous instances. Sir Walter Scott and Sir James Mackintosh were greatly inferior in classical scholarship to many we could name, who can scarcely write grammatical English. Of Jeffrey, Bulwer, Cooper, and Irwin, the same is true. Few men write better English, or express themselves more vigorously, than William Cobbett, who is totally unversed in Greek and Latin. The same was true of Thomas Paine. And some of the most correct and fascinating writers of the day are females, who are also strangers to the ancient classics.*

Shall we be told, that our references here are only to individuals possessed of native talents sufficiently powerful to raise them to distinction, *without* the aid of classical attainments; but that *with* such aid, they would have been much more distinguished? We reply, that this argument, so constantly used on occasions like the present, and deemed so satisfactory, is much more specious than solid. Indeed, it appears to us to be wanting in solidity altogether. To say that the individuals referred

* In one respect, we have an infinite advantage over our opponents. Ours is the *positive*, theirs the *negative* side of the question. A single proof from us, therefore, is paramount to all the negations they can offer. But we have furnished sundry proofs, in mentioning the names of several individuals who have become accomplished writers and speakers, without a knowledge of Greek and Latin. We consider our opinion, therefore, fully established. The maxim that the whole is greater than a part, is not more so.

to would, by the aid of Greek and Latin, have had greater power, and would therefore have attained more celebrity, is *to assert*, not *to prove*. It is to hazard a conjecture on a point which reason and experiment alone can decide. We should be justified, therefore, in resorting to a counter assertion, and saying, in reply to it, that they would not. But we must not deal in empty contradiction, although we are contending with empty supposition. Our business is to reason, not barely to deny.

The question is not, Whether Shakspeare, Moliere, Franklin, Washington, and others, would have been benefited by such an early and general education, as would have disciplined and strengthened all the faculties of their minds. We believe they would. The point to be settled is, Whether the study of the dead languages would have bestowed that education? and we believe it *would not*. Or the question may be, Could not the requisite instruction and training have been acquired without those languages? We think it could.

We repeat, that an acquaintance with Greek and Latin does not teach its possessor to observe, think, or analyze. Some of the most accurate and successful observers, and most vigorous thinkers, are destitute of it, while many who have it are very feeble in these respects. Nor does it teach him to *read;* because he can read the modern languages without it. So can he, without it, listen to lectures, conversation, and other forms of oral communication. But these are the chief channels through which information is acquired. It neither aids him, then, in collecting knowledge, nor in reflecting on it, preparing it for practical purposes, and then applying it. If it improves power in any thing, it is in expressing his ideas, when formed, in suitable language. As already stated, it disciplines his faculty of language alone. But that is comparatively an humble faculty, and constituted but little of the mental greatness and power of such men as Shakspeare, Franklin, and Washington. It only aided in manifesting that power. Their superiority arose chiefly from the great strength and activity of their faculties of observation, reflection, combination, and judgment. It consisted in the general vigour and compass of their genius; and neither Greek nor Latin could have enlarged or strengthened that.* To have attempted the invigoration of such minds by such means would have been like an effort to add to the might of the eagle, by improving a single pinion of his wing. To write or speak powerfully is the result of powerful conception and thought, of which words are but the drapery; while the use of graceful, accurate, and classical language is compatible with feeble thinking. Hence many books, exceedingly limited in matter, are written in a pure and pleasing style. The mere cultivation of language, therefore, by the study of Greek and Latin, makes but an humble element of a complete modern education, and adds but little to mental development. It could not have increased, in any useful

* Innumerable instances might be adduced to show, that much ancient learning may be possessed to very little purpose. Indeed, of mere book-learning, whether ancient or modern, the same is true. It is altogether insufficient to make a great man—especially a *practical* one. It has been already observed, that some of the greatest practical men that have appeared—improvers, inventors, and discoverers, both in science and the arts—have had but little learning of any kind, and none at all in Greek and Latin; but they have been all devoted readers of the book of nature, by observation and reflection. Their knowledge was, therefore, strictly their own; and most of their intellectual faculties were competently exercised and strengthened in acquiring and using it. In the acquisition of knowledge *by reading*, the faculties are exercised comparatively in a very moderate degree, and therefore but slightly strengthened and improved. Learning fills the mind but does not invigorate it. Unless, therefore, the knowledge attained by reading, be seriously reflected on, and severely tested by bringing it to the standard of nature, the mental faculties are but little benefited by it. Hence, one who reads much, and thinks but little, is called, in form of disrespect, a *book-worm*. It is often said that reading makes a full man, conversation a ready man, and writing an accurate one. To this it may be safely added, that, without observation and reflection, neither books, conversation, nor writing, nor the three united, can ever make a man great or efficient. That they may be invigorated, and rendered available for high purposes, the faculties must be suitably exercised; and it can scarcely be too often repeated, that the proper exercise of them can be derived only from the study of nature.

L

or even perceptible degree, the power or renown of either the philosopher who disarmed the thunder-cloud, the hero who achieved the freedom of a continent, or the chief magistrate who governed a nation with consummate wisdom. Nor can it ever strengthen the feeble-minded. It can never confer distinction, in things of moment, on those who *might* not have been distinguished without it. If it serves as an occasional ornament, it can do nothing more; and to do even that consistently with taste, it must be used but seldom. A brief analysis will shew how limited an element of a modern education a knowledge of Greek and Latin constitutes. Let it be given.

To be liberal and complete, the education of an American or an Englishman must include the following branches of knowledge. The pupil must be taught to read and speak his native tongue, and to write. On his attainment in these branches, it will not be contended that Greek and Latin have any influence. He must, also, be instructed in arithmetic, book-keeping, algebra, mathematics in its several subdivisions, experimental philosophy, and astronomy. With the knowledge of these, again, the ancient languages have no connexion. But our pupil's course of instruction is yet far from being complete. He must be versed in logic, general history, chronology, geography, chemistry, mineralogy, botany, natural history, political economy, mental philosophy (including the science of morals), and belles-lettres (including philosophical grammar, composition, rhetoric, taste, and criticism); and he ought to have an acquaintance with natural religion. Nor is it less important that he should know something of the structure, functions, dependencies, and relations of the human body. The entire neglect of this branch of science, in our seats of learning, is a fault, not to call it a serious evil. Not only would the study of it further enlighten and liberalize the mind, by exhibiting to it one of the most beautiful specimens of the wisdom of creation; but the knowledge thus acquired might be turned to an invaluable account in the management of education and the preservation of health.

So numerous are the elements of a complete modern education, to which a few others might be added; and in the attainment of only one of them does a knowledge of Greek and Latin afford any facility. We allude to belles-lettres. Will any one contend that it aids, also, in historical researches? We reply, In a very limited degree; and only in those departments of history which are least useful. Nor do we hesitate to express our belief, that, as far as philosophical grammar, composition, rhetoric, and taste are concerned, belles-lettres, also, may be as successfully cultivated without its aid as with it. In other words, scholars, who have never studied the ancient languages, may speak and write the English tongue as correctly, gracefully, and classically, and with as much eloquence and power, as those who have. That an acquaintance with Greek and Latin aids in mere biblical criticism, especially as relates to ancient works, is not denied. But that attainment is comparatively of little value. It renders the scholar somewhat more learned; but it does not increase his practical power, except on a few points, which are more curious than useful.

The English language is a compound of three others; the Saxon, which is its root, and the Greek and Latin, which, besides adding to its copiousness, variety, and force, have improved it in elegance and some other qualities. When it was in its infancy, its amount of words being incomplete, its construction and spelling not matured, and considerable changes constantly occurring in it, a knowledge of the tongues out of which it was formed was necessary to the scholar—of the Saxon,* as

* An acquaintance with the Saxon, even now, is as necessary to a thorough knowledge of English, as an acquaintance with Greek and Latin. Yet nobody dreams of studying Saxon. The reason is obvious. Custom has not rendered it fashionable. Thus is the *parent-stream* of our knowledge neglected as useless, while two mere *feeders* are pronounced *essential*, and years are spent in acquiring a knowledge of them.

well as of others. It was then a dependent and imperfect language, unequal to the wants of science and letters, and needed, therefore, further cultivation; but at present the case is different. It is now as mature as Greek or Latin, and has as much of an independent existence. It is in its minority no longer. Its structure and principles are established, its meaning is defined, and its origin pointed out in well-prepared dictionaries,—and its literature, the most extensive in the world, is as highly finished as any other; nor, except as may relate to a few technical terms, does it seem likely to receive any further increase *directly* from Greek or Latin. It has already drained those languages of all it wants for common use, and it will be itself the source of the chief additions and improvements it may hereafter receive. It might be easily shown that it contains already words enough to serve as the source of any verbal additions that may be necessary hereafter for the expression of new modifications of thought; and the process of forming new words from its present stock is easy and familiar.* A thorough knowledge of it, therefore, may be acquired by a sufficient cultivation of *itself alone,* without the least aid from the study of any other tongue. Dictionaries will give the true meaning and derivation of words: well-pre-

---

* For ample instruction on this point, see Webster's quarto Dictionary, article GRAMMAR, head DERIVATION. The occasional formation of new English words may be a matter of convenience, and perhaps of elegance; but it can never be *necessary*. Certainly no ground is discoverable, from which the necessity can arise. It might be readily demonstrated, that, *newly discovered objects excepted*, no idea or form of thought can present itself to the mind, which may not be clearly expressed in our language, with its present stock of words, in perhaps a *hundred different ways*. In proof of this, it rarely, if ever, happens that the same thought is clothed in the same words by any two original writers or speakers. Such is the copiousness of our mother-tongue. The number of different combinations that may be formed out of its seventy or eighty thousand words, is beyond the power of man to compute, or even fancy. If it be not *infinite*, it approaches so near it, that the line of separation cannot be imagined, much less shewn.

pared grammars will teach the structure and philosophy of it; the study of the best English authors, under competent instructors, will form a correct taste in it; and diligent and persevering practice in speaking and composition will confer excellence in both. In fine, the philosophical and practical study of the English tongue, *by itself*, carried to the extent, and executed with the thoroughness it deserves, may be made to produce more highly accomplished English writers than have yet appeared. We have said the study of English " *by itself*," because the cultivation of one language cannot improve a scholar in the knowledge of another. The study of the French gives no aid in forming an acquaintance with German, nor the study of the latter in acquiring a knowledge of Spanish; nor can the mere cultivation of Greek and Latin contribute to the formation of a finished English scholar.* He who would understand thoroughly either a language or any thing else, must *especially* study it.

* We wish to be clearly understood on this point. We do not deny that an acquaintance with Greek and Latin may make the possessor of it a more erudite English scholar than he could be without it. On the contrary, we acknowledge that it may. It will give him a more accurate knowledge of the etymology and roots of the language. That sort of knowledge, however, is greatly over-rated. Even to the writer and the orator it is much more curious than useful; and, in the transaction of affairs, whether public or private, its value is still less. It does not necessarily and certainly teach either the meaning, spelling, or pronunciation of words. They are greatly influenced by custom and fashion, and are, therefore, far from being stable and uniform. The history of the English language, for the last two or three centuries, proves this. In fine, a mere knowledge of its derivation does not, in one case in ten thousand, create a greater fitness to use the English tongue to the highest and best effect, than can be attained without it. Besides, our best dictionaries teach the etymology of our principal words, to an extent sufficient for all useful purposes. The Greek, the most perfect of languages, had no mother-tongue to which it could be traced. Hence it was studied as an original. And so may the English, *in its present condition*; and be made as rich, elegant and powerful a medium for the expression of feeling and the utterance of thought, as was ever possessed by Greece or Rome. The well-known fact, that many erudite Hellenists and Latinists are very defective in their know-

Let two youths, equal in capacity, be educated, one of them perfectly in English, and the several branches of science heretofore indicated, without Greek or Latin, and the other after the mode usually pursued in the seats of learning in England and the United States; let this experiment be fairly made, and we hazard nothing in saying that, at the age of twenty, the student of English will be far the more accomplished, both in science and in polite literature. He will surpass the other, as a writer and a speaker, in every point of excellence. The reason is plain. All his faculties have been invigorated, and taught to work; his mind has been well stored with knowledge, by cultivating the sciences; his thorough study of English, united to his familiarity with the best authors in it, has formed his taste; and long and steady practice in composition and speaking has given him a ready and entire command of his resources. In the mean time, the faculties of the other have been but *partially* exercised. Too much time has been consumed in the study of language, but not of the English language. That has been neglected for the sake of ancient literature; or an attempt has been made to learn it through the medium of that literature, and has failed, as it always must. The consequence of all this is, that neither is the mind of the pupil well supplied with knowledge, nor are his powers of expressing what he possesses, either in writing or in speaking, matured.

But what is true of *one* on this subject, is true of *many*. The two scholars here referred to, therefore, may be considered the representatives of indefinite numbers; nor do we hesitate to believe that, of two rival colleges, one bestowing the complete English education here designated, and the other adhering to the system of instruction usually pursued in our country, the former would have a striking

---

ledge of English, and that many others are actually versed in it, speaking and writing it with elegance and force, without an acquaintance with Greek and Latin, proves conclusively the point we are contending for—*that a knowledge of the dead languages is not essential to the thorough cultivation of all the faculties of the mind.*

superiority in the distinction and practical usefulness of its pupils. We regret to add our belief that, as Greek and Latin are now taught in the United States, the time devoted to the study of them is, in a great majority of cases, thrown away. The attainment made in them is too superficial to be creditable or in any way useful.

Are we asked, Whether we would abandon the study of the dead languages altogether? We answer, No; but we would reduce greatly the number of those who should engage in the study of them; and those who might thus engage should become thoroughly versed in them. We would have no smatterers—no linguists *in name*— but accomplished Greek and Latin scholars. They should be scholars *by profession*. And one such could do more good, in applying the ancient languages to the only useful purposes they are calculated to subserve, than the entire phalanx of those shallow Hellenists and Latinists who swarm so thickly in Europe and America. We say "Europe;" for, in a majority of cases, classical attainment *there* is not much better than with ourselves. But few critical Greek and Latin scholars can be found any where. They are probably most numerous in Germany. We shall only add, on this point, that no one should be made to toil for years in the study of classical learning, unless his faculty of language is of a high order. If it be not so, his toils will be irksome to himself, and useless to others. This distinction between a fitness and an unfitness to learn languages, though highly important, is rarely made, because the constitution of the mind, creating an aptitude for some studies, and an inaptitude for others, is understood by but few of the teachers of youth. The general notion is, that a pupil who masters one branch of study with facility, can with equal facility master all others; and that if he fails to do so, it is because he is inattentive to them. Yet facts of hourly occurrence prove its fallacy. It is owing to this preposterous practice of attempting to train in the same way minds which nature has cast in different moulds, and marked with striking diversities, that many young men, possessing fine talents for other branches of knowledge, but a weak faculty of language, have become disgusted with the drudgery of classical study, and abandoned their education. Nor is this abandonment the only evil connected with the case. A youth, under these circumstances, leaves college with a loss of reputation. Because he does not learn Latin and Greek, he is accounted either idle and dissipated, or so dull as to be unfit for any useful exertion of mind. Thus is he discouraged, underrated, and perhaps ruined. These things should be looked to and remedied; and we are confident that the period is approaching when they will be. A correct understanding of the constitution and powers of the human mind, generally diffused, especially among the directors of seats of instruction, will be the commencement of a new and brilliant era in the work of education.

The belief is general, that to all young men destined to the professions of Divinity, Law, and Medicine, the study of Greek and Latin is indispensable—at least, that it is peculiarly useful. We decline offering any remarks on the preparations deemed necessary for the former of these callings; but, as relates to the two latter, we are compelled to say, that we consider the opinion referred to erroneous. In no respect does a knowledge of the ancient classics facilitate the study of law or medicine, except on the score of technical language; and that can be learned from professional lexicons, in less than a tenth part of the time usually devoted to classical studies. An acquaintance with the professional phraseology of law*

---

* Shall we be told, in form of an objection, that certain law-books contain many scraps of Latin, which the members of the Bench and Bar should be able to understand? We reply, that this constitutes no objection to the principle we are contending for. Let the Latin quotations be translated, as they ought to be, that the pedantry and mysticism of the profession may have an end. It is neither creditable nor fair to conceal, under cover of a dead tongue, any thing essential to the administration of justice. Besides, proof can be given that the objection here stated has no weight,—at least that the obstacle said to be created by scraps of Latin in law-books can be easily surmounted. Chief Justice Marshall, one of the ablest jurists of the age—we might

and medicine *might* be acquired in a short time, as a distinct exercise; but the better way would be, for the student to attain it gradually from his lexicon, during the progress of his professional studies. The portion of time consumed by this would be inconsiderable; and the meaning of terms would be fixed in the mind more firmly than in any other way. The pupil's lexicon *must* be his oracle, whether he learn technical language as a study collateral to that of his profession, or previously through the medium of Greek and Latin. To no other interpreter can he have recourse. There is, however, a wide difference between the two methods. The oracle must be consulted a hundred times in the latter, for each single time it will need to be consulted in the former. We may safely add, that of those who have read Greek and Latin preparatory to the study of law or medicine, nineteen out of twenty are still obliged to consult their lexicons for the precise meaning of technical terms. In truth, every one is.

Shall we be charged with a disposition to abridge the course of education preparatory to the study of law and medicine, and render it more defective than it is already? The charge would be unfounded. We would greatly enlarge and improve the course, but not by saddling it with a devotion of years to the learning of words, which will be afterwards but rarely used. Instead of this, substantial *things* should be studied, which would give exercise and strength to every faculty of the mind, and store them with valuable matter. The candidates for both professions should have a perfect knowledge of English, and be well versed in history, and in the ele-

---

add, of any age—never received what can be correctly called a classical education, and is not therefore indebted to the ancient languages for his knowledge of law. If he ever acquired any knowledge of Greek or Latin, it was a mere smattering, in a common grammar-school, which was of no service to him. Most of his brothers received what is called a "classical education;" yet, without this advantage, he has towered above them all. He is, moreover, an able writer of his mother-tongue, and has been an orator of high standing.

ments of all the modern sciences. They should have an *intimate and comprehensive acquaintance with nature;* and those educated for medicine should be instructed in French, Italian, and German. Why in these languages? Because they abound in medical works, some of them very valuable, which have not been translated into English, and many of which never will be. Besides, numerous discoveries and improvements in medicine are first recorded in those languages, and ought to be immediately known to British and American physicians. Respecting the necessity of an acquaintance with the modern languages of continental Europe to lawyers, we are not prepared to speak. All statesmen, at least, who may go abroad on diplomatic missions, or in other public capacities, should be prepared to speak and write in French, if not in other foreign tongues. In fine, every youth destined to public life, or to the profession of medicine, should receive a well-finished liberal education, embracing a knowledge of two or three modern languages, and of the elements of all the sciences. Above all, he should be taught to exercise his own talents on the knowledge he may possess. Without this, attainment is but lumber.

To complete this course of instruction and training will occupy the time of the most highly-gifted youth, from his sixth until his eighteenth or twentieth year. Nor do we hesitate to believe, that the adoption of such a plan of education would usher in an era of professional, literary, and scientific splendour, such as the world has never witnessed. The study of the sciences would furnish the matter of knowledge, and give strength and activity to the *whole mind,* while the due cultivation of modern language would improve the power and all other qualities of expression, both in writing and speaking.

It has been often said, that the chief reason why British surpass American writers, in style and manner, is that they are better versed in classical literature. This is a mistake. The superiority of the British writers arises from their being better versed in *English literature.* In other words, they cultivate with more care, and to a greater extent, *the art of composition,*—for it is as real an art, as the making of razors and penknives; and it must be brought to perfection in the same way, by constant practice, and a determination to excel. So must every other pursuit. Many Englishmen have long been writers, *by profession*, and have spent their lives in improving themselves in the knowledge and use of their mother-tongue. Hence their attainment of a fine style —not because they had learned Greek and Latin at school —nor because they had in their eye, when writing, a Greek or Latin model. He who dwells in recollection on ancient literature, when composing in English, will never excel in style. It is but recently that any Americans have begun to practise authorship as a profession; and, as far as the experiment has been carried, they have no cause to be disheartened. Without being any better versed in Greek and Latin than formerly, they write English much better, because they pursue the art with more care and constancy; and should they persevere in it to the proper extent, as many of them no doubt will, they will equal in time the best British writers. Nor will they owe their success to a closer familiarity with the ancient languages, but to a more intimate acquaintance with their native tongue, and a more perfect command of their own powers. It has been already stated, that nothing can be thoroughly understood without being attentively studied as a *special subject*. To this it may be added, that there are few things which may not be mastered in that way. It is therefore that we earnestly desire to see the English language more strictly cultivated. By that means alone can it ever be written and spoken in the full perfection of which it is susceptible; and that course will complete the work. To ensure the completion, however, the language must be studied as a *simple tongue*, having a form and genius especially its own; not as a mixture of three other tongues, assimilated to each, yet identified with neither. While cultivated in the latter mode, it will be hybridous and defective. The Greek is accounted the most perfect of languages; and for this it is no doubt much indebted to its *self-dependent* character. It is not a mixture of several tongues. In their attempts to improve it, therefore, and use it in the most perfect manner, its cultivators had not their attention distracted by collateral and interfering claims. They studied and practised Greek alone, without looking to any higher source. Hence the success of their long-continued effort.

As relates to English, the same would be true. If studied and improved, in a distinct capacity, it would be brought, more certainly than in any other way, to the highest perfection it can ever attain. Hence we would rejoice to see an Institute* established, with a sufficient number of able professors, and all the necessary means of instruction, where nothing would be taught but modern science and modern language. But they should be taught in perfection. We believe that such an institution would be amply patronized, and would produce in time the happiest effects. The experiment would at least solve the problem, How far a knowledge of Greek and Latin is indispensable as an element of a liberal education? and the solution would be useful, by settling a

* As far as we are informed on the subject, the only *approach* toward an institution of this kind, made in the United States, is the "High School" of Boston. Yet *it is only* an approach. As far, however, as the experiment has been carried, it has been eminently successful, and has opened the most flattering prospect for something more perfect. In that institution, nothing is taught but the elements of science and modern languages. Nor are those educated in it intended for what are called the "learned professions." They are designed chiefly to become merchants, mechanics, and English teachers. Notwithstanding this, we are told that when they meet, as they sometimes do, the pupils of Harvard, in any form of intellectual strife, they occupy no inferior ground, but appear to great advantage. No stranger can tell, except perhaps from an occasional scrap of Greek or Latin, who is from the "High School," and who from the University. We doubt not that the first fair experiment of a complete English and scientific education will be made in New England, where most of our important improvements begin; and we deem it exceedingly desirable that it be made soon.

controversy which, without the experiment, threatens to be interminable.

Finally, were the Greek and Roman nations now in existence, possessed of no more knowledge than they had during their most enlightened periods, they would be much more benefited by studying modern languages for the sake of science, than the moderns are by studying theirs for the attainment of words. Such, we feel confident, would be their own opinion; and their conduct would conform to it. Thus would the current of education be reversed, the less enlightened people being no longer considered a model for the more enlightened to imitate.

POSTSCRIPT.

It was not until after the preceding essay was finished, that we had an opportunity to peruse, in the "American Quarterly Register," an article on the "Study of Greek Literature." Notwithstanding the zeal and scholarship, and we may add the fervid eloquence, with which the subject is there treated, our views are unshaken by any thing the writer has been enabled to advance. Unfortunately, though he has handled the matter, in his *own way*, with what some people may call ability, it is in *such* a way as can never elicit any genuine light, and therefore never lead to a satisfactory conclusion. Instead of writing philosophically, he has written rhetorically; and, instead of an analysis, has given a panegyric. He has asserted much, but proved nothing—except by authority —we mean, by the opinion of men who thought as he thinks, and were, therefore, we apprehend, very partial witnesses. Might we repose entire confidence in all he alleges—and he seems sincere in all—we would be almost induced to believe, that without an acquaintance with "Greek literature," no one could learn even to speak or write in English—certainly that no one could learn to do either with correctness or high effect. But we trust that the reverse has been established in the body of our article. The main drift of the writer's argument —if argument it might be called—consists in the allegation, that a great majority of the distinguished authors and orators of modern times have been versed in Greek literature. The truth of this has been already admitted, and a reason assigned for it, which is deemed satisfactory. That somewhat of the character of the paper in the "Register" may be the better known, we shall make a few extracts from it.

"A philosophical knowledge of English is impossible, without acquaintance with a language from which more than fourteen hundred words are derived, and if we trace etymologies through the Latin, nearly forty thousand. It is also impossible to know the compass and depth of English literature, without being scholars in Greek. The revival of classical literature, as if 'coming to create new worlds,' reduced the unformed intellectual waste to order and beauty through all Europe. It was the providence of God that commanded it, and forthwith light

'Sprung from the deep, and from her native East,
To journey through the airy gloom began.'"

We shall not offer, on this quotation, all the strictures to which it is liable. It might be sufficient to remark— and every reader of judgment will concur with us—that it has neither argument nor philosophy in it. It contains nothing but assertion, conveyed in a few flourishes of rhetoric and poetry. This, however, is not its worst fault. It is inaccurate in *fact* or *expression*, or both. Does the writer mean to say, that "forty thousand" English words are derived *immediately* from Latin words, which are again derived *immediately* from Greek? If so, he is mistaken. We profess not to know how many words Rome borrowed from Greece. But the number is far short of forty thousand. The whole catalogue of *original* Greek words—we mean Greek *roots*—does not, we believe, exceed *five or six thousand*. And if such be not our author's meaning, we are unable to detect it, so obscure is its language. The phraseology to " trace etymologies (of English) through the Latin" (to the Greek) justifies, we think, the construction we put on it.

Admitting, however, that " forty thousand" English words were derived from the Greek through the Latin, the fact would not justify the writer's inference from it. An acquaintance with Greek would not then be *essential* to a " knowledge of the philosophy of English." It would be important in its *etymology*. Strictly speaking, however, the mere *derivation* of a language constitutes no *very material* portion of its *philosophy*, much less the *whole* of it. It makes a part of its *history*, and very little more.* Were the case otherwise, what would become

---

* A brief examination of the subject can scarcely fail to convince us, that a knowledge of the etymology of English words neither contributes materially to our ready and correct understanding of them, nor facilitates our application of them to their highest and best purposes, in writing and speech. These ends can be attained only by associating and conversing with individuals of education and taste, by consulting our dictionaries, by studying carefully the best English writers, and by frequently exercising ourselves in composition and speaking, always taking care that the language we use be select and accurate. And, by a steady perseverance in this course, we can attain to the highest command of English, as a medium of expression, without studying the languages from which it is derived. That this is true, appears satisfactorily from the following analysis.

The English, as heretofore mentioned, is derived from three other languages, Saxon, its parent stream, and Latin and Greek, in the character of feeders. That a knowledge of the roots of Saxon English, then, is as necessary as a knowledge of the roots of that which is furnished by Latin and Greek, will not be denied. But that neither is *necessary*, facts innumerable concur to prove.

The following words are of Saxon origin; and no English scholar of the most ordinary education misunderstands them, or applies them incorrectly, in either writing or speaking. On the contrary, he has as full and perfect a command of them as the most accomplished Latin, Greek, or Saxon scholar.

Tale, hand, handle, finger, fang, speech, snake, snail, snug, crum, smut, hurt, hunger, din, wake, watch, grave, groove, storm, day, witch, wicked, field, heaven, earth, if.

of the philosophy of the Greek language itself, with whose *parent* tongue we have no acquaintance? What of the philosophy of the Hebrew, which some suppose to

These words, we repeat, no one ever misunderstands or misapplies. Yet how few are acquainted with their etymology; and how little will any one be benefited, in using them, by being told that they are derived as follows!

Tale, from—Tellan—to tell.
Hand, from—Hentan—to take hold of.
Handle, from—Handell, a diminutive from the same root.
Finger, from—Fenger, a holder or catcher, which comes again from Fengan—to catch or hold.
Fang, from the same verb, Fengan.
Speech, from—Spæce—to speak.
Snake, from—Snican—to creep.
Snail, from—Snægal—a little creeper, which is again from the same verb, Snican.
Snug, from—Snican—to crawl or sneak.
Crum, from—Grymman—to break.
Smut, from—Smytan—to pollute.
Hurt, from—Hyrtian—to injure.
Hunger, from—Hyngrian—to eat.
Din, from—Dynan—to make a noise.
Wake,
Watch, } from Wecan—to wake or watch.
Grave,
Groove, } from Grafan—to dig.
Storm, from—Styrmian—to agitate or shake.
Day, from—Dægian—to shine.
Witch,
Wicked, } from—Wiecian—to enchant, or injure by poison or sorcery.
Field, from—Fellan—to fell or cut down; because the timber is cut down in a field.
Heaven, from—Heofen—to raise, because heaven is supposed to be on high.
Earth, from—Erith—ploughed; because the earth is a ploughed place.
If or *Gif*, from—Gifan—to give; *if* signifying *give*, or *grant*. Thus, *if* a thing be so, is tantamount, in meaning, to *give* or *grant* that it be so.

Of all words of Saxon-English the same may be affirmed. No English scholar misunderstands or misapplies them; nor is he benefited, in making use of them, by a knowledge of their derivation. An attempt to remember their derivation, when in the act of employing them,

be the primitive language of man? Must we abandon the study of the philosophy of those two languages, because we are ignorant of their roots? The writer will not say would but encumber the memory of a writer or speaker, and impede the operations of his mind.

Of words of Latin-English the same is true. A knowledge of their etymology gives no appreciable facility in their employment, or in the accurate understanding of them. No tolerable English scholar ever mistakes the meaning or use of the following terms:—

Post, in the ground—military *post*—*post* under government—*post*-office—*post*-chaise—to travel *post*—*post*, for horses—*apposite, opposite, composite, impost, compost, deposit, depot, repose, compose, pause, position, composition, deposition.*

Yet but few English scholars know that all these terms and different forms of expression have, as their root, the Latin verb *Pono*, to place. Nor does the Latin scholar pay the least regard to this root, when he is making use of them in writing or speech. He conforms to *custom*, which here, and in every other case, is what the poet pronounces it,

"Et jus, et norma loquendi"—

the law and rule of speech. Again,

Fact, effect, defect, perfect, prefect, fit, feat, defeat, counterfeit, forfeit, surfeit, benefit, profit, and several similar words, come from the Latin root *Facio*. Yet what mere English scholar knows this; or what Latin one troubles himself to think of it, when he is employing the derivative terms? Palpably none. Yet every one understands the terms, and applies them correctly. Once more.

Promise, compromise, committee, pretermit, premiss, remiss, surmise, demise, mission, commission, omission, are all derived from *Mitto*; and *quest, inquest, request, conquest, acquest, bequest, exquisite, requisite, perquisite, question,* and several others, have their origin in *Quæro*. But does the English scholar know all this? Does he sustain any injury in the exercise of his powers from not knowing it? or does the Latin scholar always refer to it when he meets with these terms in reading, or uses them in writing or speaking? To each of these questions the correct answer is, No. Of all Latin-English the same is true. Nor is it less so of Greek-English, as might be easily shewn, were it allowable in us to dwell any longer on the subject. Thus,

Philanthropy, misanthropy, anarchy, monarchy, hierarchy, heptarchy, archangel, archbishop, archdeacon, archetype, oligarchy, theocracy, aristocracy, democracy, panorama, diorama, cosmodrama, baptize, are all correctly understood and employed, both by the learned and unlearned, without any reference to their Greek origin.

But, admitting the importance of an acquaintance with the etymo-

so. Wherefore, then, is an acquaintance with Greek essential to a "knowledge of the philosophy of English?" It is left to the writer to render an answer, under a conviction that he will not be able to frame a satisfactory one. We fear he has not taken a correct view of what constitutes the philosophy of language. In the compass and multifariousness of philosophical grammar, etymology forms but a very limited point. Another quotation.

"The old English literature, the rich, massy architecture of the true English mind, is all Greek in spirit. In habitual communion with Grecian intellect, the ruling minds of England, in the first era of her true greatness, grew to a majestic intellectual stature. The student of that age finds himself in a sphere, where his emotions are somewhat like those of Brennus and his soldiers, when they advanced into the midst of the hall, around which the venerable priests and senators of Rome, in their robes of state, and white flowing beards, and the sceptre of office in their hands, were seated in silent dignity. Mas-

---

logy of Latin and Greek-English, a much shorter and easier route may be opened to it than that now pursued. A knowledge of the *original* Greek and Latin *roots* is all that is necessary as a key to what is wanted;' and that can be attained in less than a fifth part of the time usually consumed in the study of those languages. Two works are already extant in Great Britain which are alone sufficient to communicate the knowledge required. Their titles are, "THE STUDENT'S MANUAL; being an Etymological and Explanatory Vocabulary of Words derived from the Greek;" and "AN ETYMOLOGICAL AND EXPLANATORY DICTIONARY OF WORDS DERIVED FROM THE LATIN; being a Sequel to the Student's Manual." Of these the former is already in its fifth edition, and the latter in its third; a circumstance demonstrative of their usefulness and popularity. By regular exercises on the words they contain, being *roots* alone, English scholars attain, in a short time, all that is requisite toward the etymology of their native tongue, so far as it is derived from Greek and Latin.

That these vocabularies, or others like them, will be extensively adopted, as means of education, can scarcely be doubted; nor do we hesitate to believe, that, in time, even *they* will go out of use, and English dictionaries be so prepared as to supply their places. And we further believe, that the latter plan will be an important improvement on all preceding ones.

ter spirits are around him, their aspect commanding and sublime, their dress heavy with the magnificence of former ages, their movements of godlike majesty, their features shining with the expression of a great indwelling soul."

Were we inclined to be severe in our animadversions on this extract, we should be justified in using, as respects it, the saw of Napoleon, " From the sublime to the ridiculous is but a single step." We do not say that the writer has taken that step; but, should the reader say or think so, he has our permission to do it. We shall not contradict him. The whole concern, matter, style, and manner is no bad specimen of one of the ebullitions of a youthful orator, in his maiden speech, on the fourth of July. It is fustian throughout. Is the writer actually enamoured of that fashion and style of literary " dress," which is " heavy with the magnificence of former ages ?" in more intelligible words, which is stiff and formal from transposition, and studded all over with classical conceits, and many-coloured scraps of Greek and Latin, after the manner of Burton's " Anatomy of Melancholy." Would the return of that style of writing rejoice him ? If so, we envy not his taste. We had much rather witness, in personal costume, the return of stiff brocades, gaudy stomachers, slash-sleeves, three-cornered hats, bag-wigs, and laced waistcoats and breeches; because we think literary harlequinism worse than that of bodily clothing. As the writer is such an admirer of ancient literature, we wonder that he forgets the caution of the Roman satirist against the *purpureus pannus, verba sesquipedalia*, and other like ornaments. In the literature of the age he so peculiarly delights in, much of this antiquated decoration, intermingled with the quaint conceits of the time, presents itself. We prefer simplicity, ease, and flexibility in all sorts of dress, mental as well as corporeal; and hence our dislike of starch, buckram, and patch-work. We would as soon see our warriors cased in steel armour, as our English writers in the garb worn by them during the reign of Elizabeth and her father.

The writer in the "Register" alleges, that, "in the degenerate age of Charles the Second, it was the profound classical scholars of England who preserved her virtuous literature from extinction." This is true; and the reason of it has been already given. All the educated men of the time were classical scholars; and such only could be the guardians of literature. The writer recites the names of nearly forty individuals, to whom he does homage as the curators of learning; and adds, "The *classical* erudition of these men gave them a reach of thought, and a grasp of knowledge, which makes *this age look back on them with wonder.*" This eulogy is extravagant, and speaks only the over-wrought admiration of its author. The personages referred to were highly distinguished; but they were *men*, and no more to be *wondered at*, either by this age or by any other, than hundreds of individuals who have flourished at a later period. Besides, no competent judge of the human intellect will contend that it was their " classical erudition" which made them great. Nature formed them to be great; their faculties were strengthened and trained, and their minds enriched with the science of the day; and their attainments in literature, whether ancient or modern, enabled them only to manifest their greatness in writing and speech. The author's statement to the contrary of this is perfectly gratuitous. Nor, for reasons assigned in the body of this article, is it founded in fact. Language, and the modes of using it, are the *effect* of ideas and thought, not their *cause*. Intellectual views are formed first, and then words are provided to express them. *Ideas* may exist without *speech*; but, were there no ideas, there would be no speech, because there would be neither use nor foundation for it. There would be nothing to speak about. To contend, then, that mere language enriches, polishes, and strengthens the mind, and confers lustre on those who possess it, is to invert the order of nature. Knowledge, we repeat, is the fountain of speech; not speech of knowledge. " Out of the fulness of the heart the mouth speaketh." And this is as true of the Greek language as of any other. Grecian superiority in mental cultivation was not the effect of Grecian literature. It was its cause. The ancient Greeks were much better versed in their own language and literature than any moderns are. But were they therefore greater? more illustrious, we mean, for the amount, power, and usefulness of their attainments? Far from it. On the contrary, they were greatly inferior. Moderns might be named whom the Greeks would have deified on account of their lustre. Franklin, a stranger to the Greek alphabet, was one of them. Of Fulton the same may be safely affirmed. Another quotation will shew, with still greater force, the fanatical rhapsody with which an attempt is made to exalt, above every other mental product, English literature, said to be cast in a Greek mould, and to be instinct with a Greek spirit.

" No other nation possesses any thing to be compared for its richness to our English literature of the seventeenth century. It is surprising, that with such materials out of which to build up a strong and symmetrical intellect, the individual as well as general mind of our own age should be comparatively so narrow and misshapen." * * * " The student" (*of the present degenerate day*) " does not make himself familiar with the productions of the old English mind; he does not choose his companions, his moral and intellectual friends, out of them. Their contents are imperishable thoughts and principles, not facts merely, and it will not avail to take up a volume, read it cursorily, and then throw it aside to have the attention distracted by the trash upon a modern book-shelf—they must be read and reflected on; they contain not mere knowledge, but wisdom. Their spirit must be taken by habitual communion into the mind, to interpenetrate and imbue it, and become, as it were, a part of the intellectual self-consciousness. They should be so studied as to constitute for the soul an atmosphere of thought, by which it may become invigorated for original action, inhaling it, as it were, unconsciously and freely, like the play of the lungs in the mountain air. In such an atmosphere the mind *grows*, its energies are roused, it feels its own power, and moves like a warhorse on the eve of battle. The feeling of excitement and exultation which powerful thought thus produces, is discipline, discipline of the best kind; and this is the reason why the strongest minds have been the greatest classical enthusiasts."

This paragraph was no doubt intended by its author to be matchless alike in *profundity* and *sublimity*—to be, in matter and diction, like Jupiter Tonans's threatened plunge of any disobedient brother god:

> " As far beneath the infernal centre hurled,
> As from that centre to the ethereal world."

We give it to the reader as we find it, without guaranteeing its goodness or badness, truth or falsity; for we profess to know but little about it. It is mostly beyond our comprehension. In plain terms, it is empty bombast—a mere tissue of words, calculated to injure, rather than subserve, any thing attempted to be sustained by it. In the *most* intelligible, if not the *only* intelligible, part of it, the statement it makes is unfounded. It is far from being true, that the " strongest minds have been the greatest classical enthusiasts." As heretofore intimated, the reverse is much nearer the truth. One quotation more, and adieu to the Hellenist of the " Register."

After recommending a return to " the study of the ancient Greek classics," as the only preventive of " modern degeneracy and a depraved taste," the writer adds: " Unless this be done, erudition will soon become an obsolete term. There is an evident passion to avoid hard study, and obtain every acquisition at least possible expense of thought. The unparalleled advancement of physical science has *contributed to this evil*. The study of the physical sciences demands patience and skill in the observation of the external universe, it requires ingenuity in detecting the secret affinities and operations of nature, but it does not turn the mind in upon itself, it does not tend to make a man inwardly *thoughtful;* it has a *contrary tendency."*

In some respects this is the most censurable extract we have made. The views it virtually inculcates are hostile alike to the progress of knowledge, and to sound taste. The cultivation of the natural sciences, which our author complains of as productive of evil, is infinitely useful. It is the study of things, *as God has made them,* and is therefore one of the noblest employments of the mind. That an educated man should condemn it, is matter of surprise. Its object is, to form an acquaintance with Nature *as she is.* And no one will deny that she is, to man, the *immediate oracle of truth;* the true interpreter of the language spoken, and the works performed, by the AUTHOR of truth. It is, moreover, by the study of nature alone, that the condition of man can be gradually ameliorated; for all improvements, whether in philosophy or in the arts, which administer to the comforts of life, flow directly from that source. Were the study of nature abandoned, all advancement in knowledge would be at an end; and, as nothing earthly is stationary, the movement of the general condition of society would be retrograde, until barbarism would again usurp the seat of civilization, and the " Dark Ages" return. Yet to this issue does our author's doctrine tend. And for what would he exchange the study of nature?— The cultivation of Greek literature. He would barter an acquaintance with what nature is doing *now,* for a *dreamy* knowledge—for it can be *only dreamy,* and never *vivid*—of what the Greeks were doing and thinking four or five-and-twenty centuries ago! In simple terms, he would give Greek literature a preference to the science and literature of creation; for creation has its language and literature as well as man; and none again can read them, but those who cultivate them. Shall we be told that the " Dark Ages" could not return, provided Greek literature were studied, in as much as it once dissipated them? We reply, that the phrase " Dark Ages" is comparative, and relates to a period of *greater light.* And, compared to the present period, the " Dark Ages" continue several centuries after the time of the Revival of Letters. Until the beginning of the seventeenth century, the world had but little more of light than a morning dawn. Yet Greek literature had been as thoroughly studied before that period, as it has been since. Besides, it was not Greek literature *alone* that shed a faint radiance on Christendom, during the fourteenth, fifteenth, and sixteenth centuries. The study of that was accompanied, to a moderate extent, by the study of nature. The light elicited, therefore, was the product of both. Finally, compared to the present state of the world, ancient Greece herself, notwithstanding her language and literature, was overshadowed by " Dark Ages." Away then with the empty notion, that the cultivation of that literature is the only way to prevent " modern degeneracy!" An exchange of the present condition of Christendom for that of the brightest period of ancient Greece, would be to barter improvement for " degeneracy."

But our author's doctrine violates correct taste, as well as sound philosophy. Greek literature is no more the source of poetry than of science. We have Helicons and Hippocrenes of our own, sufficient to inspire the votaries of song. Nor does Attica contain the only Parnassus, where Apollo has struck his harp, and the Muses dispensed their favours. To drop these *classical fictions*, and speak in the language of *sober reality:* The modern world possesses thousands of sources much better calculated to awaken and nourish the spirit of poetry, than the writings of either Homer or Pindar, Sophocles or Euripides—or of all of them united—Virgil, Horace, Ovid, and Lucan being added to the number. Nature is the fountain of poetry, no less than of philosophy; and she never grows old or fades. She is as fresh, and vigorous, and enchanting now, as she was when the " morning stars first sang together, and the sons of God shouted for joy." And she can inspire as glowingly—not to say divinely—and she does so.

America possesses more to inspire the poet, than either

Greece or Italy, or any other portion of Europe. We mean that she has native objects, in immeasurable abundance, better calculated to awaken fervid feeling, and swell and elevate the mind with broad and lofty conceptions, fire the imagination and fancy, and give richness and vigour to the powers of invention. Europe has nothing to compare with the solemn majesty of her rivers, lakes, and cataracts, the grandeur of her mountains, the depth and extent of her primeval forests, and the floral seas of her interminable prairies. Nor has she any thing equal to her fine sunny climate, the lofty arch and pellucid azure of her skies, and the gorgeous drapery they receive from the morning and evening clouds. Yet these are among the richest sources and subjects of poetry; all of which our author would neglect, to seek inspiration from Greek literature! Nor are we inferior to the Greeks in the poetry of human nature. Our passions are as deep and lofty, and our fitness to express them equal to theirs. We have as much heroism, patriotism, and general virtue and power, in the male character, and as much beauty and loveliness, and much more purity and intelligence, in the female. An Apollo, a Venus, an Antinous, or any other god, goddess, or human being, might be sculptured after living models in the United States, and be equal in perfection to those of Greece. We possess, moreover, spectacles of moral and political sublimity, to which the nations of antiquity were strangers.

The modern world is much more familiar than the ancient was, with all that constitutes the poetry of the ocean; and nothing can surpass that in grandeur, whether it be contemplated in the fury of a storm, or the sublimity of a calm. But the source of true mental enlargement, grand conception, and poetic inspiration, which leaves every other immeasurably behind it, is found in astronomy; more especially in the recent discoveries in it. And that belongs exclusively to the moderns. The ancient Greeks were strangers to it. The science of geography, which is also of modern growth, has done much for the expansion of the human mind. And whatever does that is favourable to poetry, in those who possess poetic faculties. Nor must we forget some of the modern works of art, with which the ancients had nothing to compare. How diminutive, in physical grandeur and sublimity, were the land and sea-fights of the Greeks, contrasted with those of the present day, by whose glare even the lightning of heaven is dimmed, and its thunders drowned in their tumultuous uproar! What, compared to commotions like these, are Homer's conflicts, even in " such wars" as his " Immortals wage?"—Absolutely not more than mice to mammoths! But these are all sources of poetic inspiration and taste. So are all things that tend to expand and elevate the mind, and fan its enthusiasm; and such influences are much more abundant now, than they were during the most splendid periods of Greece and Rome. They belong more especially to modern times. Several of them moreover are connected with the " physical sciences," which our author condemns as a source of " evil." To exchange all these for a few volumes of ancient literature, would be a miserable barter. It would be to prefer the productions of the Grecian pen to the handiwork of God! a greater error than which, no degree of infatuation can commit.

Finally, we have already admitted, that there was a time when a knowledge of the ancient classics was essential to a liberal education. But is that time to be interminable? Is the *minority* of the English language never to have an end? Is the period never to arrive when that language will be so mature and independent of its parentage as to be prepared to set up for itself? The warmest advocate for Greek and Latin will pause, before answering this question negatively. We doubt whether any one will so answer it. Within a century from this date, English will be the native tongue of upwards of three hundred millions of the human race. Must that immense population, whose number the mind is unable to grasp, still depend, and, notwithstanding its subsequent boundless increase, still continue to depend, on Greece and Rome for their intellectual nourishment?—for their literature and their mental discipline? The fancy is preposterous. As well may it be contended, that they will derive from those spots of earth their corporeal food. No; they will have a language of their own, answering to all their wants, and competent to the manifestation of all their powers. In fact, with the slight restrictions heretofore mentioned, the English and their descendants have such a language now; and the time will arrive, when to oppose this opinion will be considered as much the result of antiquated prejudice, as to advocate it now is considered the work of a spirit of innovation. Nor do we hesitate to believe, that, ages hence, when the Greek and Latin languages shall have been neglected and forgotten, English literature, in common with general and professional science, will be in a state of much higher perfection than it has yet attained. Greek and Latin are destined to become the Sanscrit of future times, known only to the antiquarian and the virtuoso; while English, in an improved condition, will be as lasting as our race.

INDEX.

ABSENCE of mind, 74.
Age when children ought to be sent to school, 37.
Air, purity of, 27, 45.
America, political strife and bitterness in, 1, 84; cleanliness neglected there, 26; gluttony in, 44; manual labour academies in, 50; dyspepsia and insanity prevalent in, 81.

Balance of the organs, 78, 120.
Bathing recommended, 27, note.
Beaumont, Dr, remarkable case reported by, 89, note.
Blood, 46, 105.
Book-learning, 161, note.
Boots and shoes, tight, 103.
Brain, not mind, improved by education, 8, 61; effect of its disease on the rest of the body, 11; its condition in childhood, 37; physical education of the, 61; a compound organ, 62; can its organs be enlarged by exercise? 65; boys with small brains unfit to be professional or scientific men, 72; equilibrium of its departments conducive to health, 78; influence of disease of the brain on digestion, 87; brains of criminals, 94; circulation of blood in the brain quickened when mind active, 105.
Buckskin inexpressibles ridiculed, 104.

Carriage-exercise, 55.
Christian religion, 64.
Classical studies, 123; whether they strengthen the intellectual faculties, 138; whether they facilitate the acquisition of modern languages, 148; whether they foster the spirit of rational freedom, 151; considered as branches of polite literature, 157; many eminent writers have been indifferent classical scholars, 158; ought not to be entirely abolished, 167; whether necessary to professional men, 168.
Cleanliness, 26, 43.
Clergymen, importance of muscular exercise to, 49, note.
Clothing, 27, 103.

Corporal punishment reprobated, 97.
Corsets, tight, very prejudicial, 107.
Cravats, tight, 104.
Criminals, brains of, 94; how they ought to be treated, 95.
Crying of infants, how far beneficial, 28.

Dancing recommended, 57.
Dark ages, 183.
Declamation beneficial, 47.
Derivation of words, 165, note. 174
Diet, 24, 43, 49.
Digestive organs, 43, 49.
Disease, predisposition to, 76.
Dress, 27, 103.
Dyspepsia, 81, 86, 110.

Eccentricity, often a prelude of madness, 74.
Education, importance of, as a means of advancing intelligence and virtue, 3; defined, 6; physical, moral, and intellectual, 9; mutual relations of these three branches, 10; nursery education, 24, 31, note, 36; moral education, 67, 95; classical education, 123; what constitutes a liberal education? 125, 162.
English literature, 132, 147, 170; of the seventeenth century, 178; English language, whence derived, 163, 174.
Equilibrium of the cerebral organs, 78; of the organs of the body, 120.
Etymology, 165, note, 174.
Example, 33.
Exercise, muscular, very beneficial, 29, 48, 49, 54; time for, 58.

Fanaticism, 74, 84.
Fencing recommended, 57.
Food, 24, 43, 49.
Freedom, spirit of, not fostered by classical learning, 151.

Grammar, universal, 143.
Greek and Latin, 123; sonorous languages, 155. See *Classical Studies*.
Greeks cultivated physical education, 12.
Grief injures digestion, 89.

INDEX.

Hereditary transmission of bodily and mental qualities, 14, *et seq.* 76.

Improvement of man to be effected by improving his brain, 64, 67, 77.
Indigestion, 81, 86, 110.
Infants, their diet, 24; cleanliness, 26; clothing, 27; respiration, 28; crying, ib.; muscular exercise, 29.
Infant-schools, 39.
Insanity, 70, 73, 74, 81.

Language, philosophy of, 142.
Latin and Greek, 123; sonorous languages, 155. See *Classical Studies.*
Lawyers, whether classical learning necessary to, 168.
Light, its beneficial influence on health, 28, 50.
Literary men, cause of their bad health, 49; indigestion of, 90.
Longevity, 78.
Lungs, 45, 110, 121.

Madness, 70, 73, 74, 81.
Manual labour academies, 50.
Marriage, 15, 18, *et seq.*
Mastication, 25.
Masturbation, 101.
Mathematics, study of, 127.
Medical men, whether classical learning necessary to, 168.
Memory, how far strengthened by classical studies, 138; philosophy of, ib.
Mercantile speculation, 85.
Millennium, 63, 77.
Mind and matter, 7, 59.
Moral sentiments sometimes indulged to excess, 73.
Moral training, 67, 95.
Mortality of different classes, 78.
Mothers, influence of their state during gestation upon their children, 23, 111; their influence on the character of their children, 35.

Nature, study of, recommended, 182.
Nursery education, 24, 31, note, 36.

Parents, influence of their health and mental qualities on those of their children, 14, *et seq.*; duty of setting a good example before their children, 33. See *Mothers.*
Passion unfavourable to longevity, 78; retards digestion, 89.
Penitentiaries, 95.

Persians cultivated physical education, 12.
Phrenology, 5, 61, 71, 75, 122.
Physical education, importance of, 11; neglected by the moderns, 12; defined, 13.
Polite literature, 157.
Precocity of mind, 37.
Predisposition to disease, how removable, 76.
Pregnancy, 23, 111.
Press, its licentiousness in America, 2.
Prison discipline, 95.

Reading, 161, note.
Religious feeling may become excessive, 74, 84.
Respiration, 28.
Riding beneficial, 55.

St Martin, Alexis, case of, 89, note.
Saxon, the main source of English words, 175.
School, children ought not to be sent too early to, 37; situation of school houses, 45; attitudes of children in, 101.
Sciences, study of, recommended, 182.
Self-pollution, 101.
Shoes and boots, tight, 103.
Siesta, 58.
Singing a beneficial exercise, 47.
Skin, 26, 43.
Sleep, 99.
Spine, distortion of the, 112.
Stays, tight, very prejudicial, 107.
Stomach complaints, 81, 86, 110.
Students, cause of their bad health, 49; indigestion of, 90.
Study, change of, beneficial, 68.
Swimming recommended, 57.
Sword exercise recommended, ib.

Talent, natural diversity of, 72.
Taste, on what it depends, 136.
Teachers, 4.
Teething, 35.
Temperature, 27.
Time for exercise, 58.
Translations may equal originals, 153.

Vaccination, 36.
Variety of studies, 68; of talent, 72.
Ventilation, 27, 45.

Women generally take too little exercise, 54; tight lacing prejudicial to, 107. See *Mothers.*

PRINTED BY NEILL & CO., OLD FISHMARKET, EDINBURGH.

www.ingramcontent.com/pod-product-compliance
Lightning Source LLC
Chambersburg PA
CBHW080437110426
42743CB00016B/3192